Mountain Peaks of the Bible

by

Rev. Bud Robinson

First Fruits Press
Wilmore, Kentucky
2015

Mountain Peaks of the Bible by Bud Robinson

Published by First Fruits Press, © 2015
Previously Published by Pentecostal Publishing Company

ISBN: 9781621711858 (print), 9781621711841 (digital)

Digital version at
http://place.asburyseminary.edu/firstfruitsheritagematerial/89/

First Fruits Press is a digital imprint of the Asbury Theological Seminary, B.L. Fisher Library. Asbury Theological Seminary is the legal owner of the material previously published by the Pentecostal Publishing Co. and reserves the right to release new editions of this material as well as new material produced by Asbury Theological Seminary. Its publications are available for noncommercial and educational uses, such as research, teaching and private study. First Fruits Press has licensed the digital version of this work under the Creative Commons Attribution Noncommercial 3.0 United States License. To view a copy of this license, visit http://creativecommons.org/licenses/by-nc/3.0/us/.

For all other uses, contact First Fruits Press

Robinson, Bud, 1860-1942.
   Mountain peaks of the Bible / by Bud Robinson.
   164 p. ; 21 cm.
   Wilmore, KY : First Fruits Press, ©2015.
   Reprint. Previously published: Louisville, KY : Pentecostal Publishing Company, ©1913.
   ISBN: 9781621711858 (pbk.).
   1. Pentecostal churches -- Doctrines. 2. Pentecostal churches – Controversial literature. 3. Typology (Theology) I. Title
DS9 .R62 2015   915.69

Cover design by Amelia Hegle

First Fruits Press
The Academic Open Press of Asbury Theological Seminary
204 N. Lexington Ave., Wilmore, KY 40390
859-858-2236
first.fruits@asburyseminary.edu
asbury.to/firstfruits

REV. BUD ROBINSON

Mountain Peaks
OF THE BIBLE

By BUD ROBINSON

Copyrighted 1913 by
PENTECOSTAL PUBLISHING COMPANY,
LOUISVILLE. KY.

INTRODUCTION.

Another book by Bud Robinson! Yes, Buddie has "just been touchin' the high places," and wants to tell you about it. You who have wept at the story of his life in Sunshine and Smiles, laughed over his Pitcher of Cream, and shouted as Lazarus came forth, will be glad to go with him to the Mountain Peaks and see what God has wrought there. There is not much in this volume to make you weep (unless you are a sinner), not much to make you laugh, but you will have an opportunity to find and enjoy a mountain-top experience, which, as Buddie says, is the best thing in this country.

CHAS. A. MCCONNELL.

DEDICATION.

I lovingly dedicate this book to my elder daughter, Little Sallie, who has been the comfort of her mamma and the joy of her father. Her life has been so pure and sweet, and the smiles on her face have been such an inspiration to her papa while he was miles away, she has encouraged him to go forward with the work of the Master, and as this book is a sketch of the mountain-top life, may the life of my precious daughter be like the sunshine on the mountain top. May her life be as pure as the dew that falls on the mountain, and may she never lose that gentleness of character and that sweetness of disposition. Her life in our home has been one of comfort and satisfaction. Her love for her mother has been so beautiful, and her kindness and confidence in her papa has been such a comfort and joy to him, that without her life would be a burden.

The little, sweet things of her baby life will cling to her father as long as he lives. When she was less than two years old, one day I lay down on the cot to take a little rest, and she wanted to go somewhere. She came in and found a razor strap, and as I had dropped off to sleep, she struck me in the face as hard as she could pound me, and as I waked out of my sleep she said, "Huddle up da, huddle up," and as I got off the cot she put up both hands and said, "Go da, go." And on another occasion I went to work out my garden, and of course she had to go and help me. I got my hoe and went to work and I sung, "Amazing grace, how sweet the sound," and hoed my beans. She got right in behind me, and when I had hoed one row and looked back, she was right behind me, and every bean that I had hoed she had pulled up, and had her hands full of the beans. As I looked back at her she smiled, and said, "Da, I am helping you work the garden." I thought that she was the smartest thing on earth, and took her to the house to let her mother see how smart our baby was.

From that day until now she has been a great helper of her papa. I think that we will get to evangelize together all over the United States, and may be all over the world. My prayers go up to our heavenly Father daily that He may use her to bless the world. While I write these words her sweet face is before me, and I see the smiles playing up and down her face, and today I dedicate her afresh to the blessed Christ, to be His and to be used for His glory and for the good of the world in which we live. Amen.

BUD ROBINSON.

THE HOLY MOUNTAINS.

The first mountain is the Mount of Worship Noah worshipping God under the first rainbow.

The Second mountain is the Mount of Sacrifice, or Abraham offering up Isaac.

The third mountain is the Mount of Fire, or the mount of commandment, or God commanding Moses to go down and deliver Israel.

The fourth mountain is the Mount of Law, or the mount of honor. No mountain was ever honored like Mt. Sinai. God and Moses stood together and talked for forty days.

The fifth mountain is the Mount of Vision, or Nebo's heights, or Moses viewing the Promised Land.

The sixth mountain is the Mount of Possession, or Caleb taking charge of Mount Hebron.

The seventh mountain is the Mount of Testing, or Elijah proving God.

The eighth mountain is the Mount of Blessing, or Christ on the mount.

The ninth mountain is the Mount of Transfiguration.

The tenth mountain is the Mount of Calvary.

The eleventh mountain is the Mount of Commission, or Christ giving the Commission to the disciples to go out and preach the gospel to all nations.

The twelfth mountain is the Mount of Ascension, or the Son of God going back to the right hand of the Father.

CHAPTER I.

MOUNT ARARAT.

The first mountain of note is the Mount of Ararat. This mountain is forever made sacred from the fact that after God had destroyed a world of God-forgetters and grace-rejecters, that after the world had been lost sight of for a year, the hills and mountains crawled out from under the flood like a lizard crawling out from under the leaves and old chestnut logs.

In the dawning of the Spring of the year, how natural it is for a boy to go out into the woods and watch the lizards crawl out from under the leaves and crawl upon the old chestnut logs and sun themselves in the air; and just now we look and behold the mountain of Ararat is crawling out from under the awful flood that has swept the face of the earth, and behold, the Ark of God is just now floating that way, and, to our surprise, she rests on the top of the mountain, and Noah sends out a dove; she returns and he waits seven days and sends her out the second time, and behold, she returns with the olive leaf in her mouth. He waits seven days longer and sends her the third time, and behold, she returns not to him. He waits seven days and removes the covering of the Ark, and the earth is dry, and he and his family and all of his flocks and herds come forth from the Ark.

And now Noah builds an altar and offers up a sacrifice to the Lord, and the Lord accepts his offering, and while Noah is holding the service, the beautiful rainbow appears, and God speaks to Noah and tells him that the rainbow in the cloud shall be His everlasting covenant; and it is not only between Noah and the Lord, but it is an everlasting covenant between God and this world. Every time we see the beautiful bow, we know that God will not destroy this world with water again.

We see by the flood that this old world has been baptized with water once, and everything that has been added to the earth from creation's morn till that day was destroyed in the flood. But the curse of the earth, for man's sake, was not removed, for after the flood the earth brought forth briers and thorns and reptiles and sickness and death.

But by and by, we are to have another baptism poured out on this old earth, and the next one is by fire, and not only that which was added to the earth is to be removed, but the **very curse** of the earth is to be burned out, and we are to look for a new heaven and a new earth, wherein dwelleth righteousness.

We see the same kind of a family coming out of the Ark that went into the Ark. We see that the stay in the Ark did not change the nature of the families that went into it, and in a short time after the flood we see the human family as far from God as they were when the flood came.

Just so we have seen men powerfully converted and then baptized with water and it looked like for a few days that they were all right and did not need the other baptism. But they had not run long till they woke up to the fact that they were in need of the second blessing as bad as this old earth needs it. By and by we get them into a red-hot holiness meeting and get them baptized with the Holy Ghost and fire and get them established.

We find that the man that built the Ark got into trouble before he got off to the upper world. He was a great man, but he needed something else to establish him, and that is what we call the last baptism. This old world has been baptized once with water and must be baptized again with fire.

The man on the road to heaven is a man that has been born twice; he has been born of the flesh and also born of the Spirit, and he has been baptized with water and he has been baptized with the Holy Ghost. You see two births and two baptisms, and the longer you look the plainer it gets to you. Well, amen! We have been accused of preaching the second blessing from all the Bible, and thank God we are guilty and don't deny the charge at all. Well amen and glory!

Another beautiful thing about the Mount of Worship is this: The lamb that Noah used in the offering was a beautiful type of the Blessed Christ. The lamb was put to death and then burnt on the altar. It was not blessed and turned loose, but it was blessed and then brought forth and the animal life was killed out of the lamb, then put on the altar. The fire was turned loose on the lamb and in the next moment the blue smoke was ascending to the clouds.

The Book says that God smelled a sweet savour going up to heaven, and He was pleased with Noah and his offering and blessed him and gave him and his sons the whole world to take possession of, and to repeople it and start the race again. That looked like a great undertaking, but the Lord was with them and blessed them and told them to be fruitful and multiply and replenish the earth. Today we look out on the teeming millions of Noah's race; he is today the grandfather of all the human family, and that makes him sure enough a grand dad. Just look at the family as it goes by and you will wonder where they all come from, and then you will remember that they all come from Noah, for he is the father of the living now, and his children have multiplied on the face of the earth until there are millions of them.

One of his last acts was to get drunk, and his grandsons are still keeping up the record of their grandfather.

While we see the holy Mount of Worship and the Ark, which represents the everlasting covenant of the Lord to His people, and the bleeding lamb, which was the type of Christ, we also see the man on the drunk and his grandsons following in the footsteps of their grandfather.

Today tens of thousands of our fellow-countrymen have forgotten the holy mountain and the bleeding lamb and the Ark of the covenant and have lost sight of everything but the wine that made the man drunk and robbed him of his honor and of his manhood, and they follow him day by day.

CHAPTER II.

MOUNT MORIAH.

We now come to the second mountain, which is the Mount of Sacrifice, and it is Mount Moriah. This is one of the mountains that the human family will hold very sacred, for it was on this mountain that our Father Abraham offered up his son Isaac on the altar as a burnt sacrifice.

The human family will never forget the man Abraham, for he was called the father of the faithful. Well, it was because he was faithful, and he never flinched one hair's breadth. Bro. H. C. Morrison says that "God called and Abraham went, and God promised and Abraham believed, and God asked and Abraham gave." I thought at the time that I heard my beloved brother say that, that it was the greatest thing I had ever heard fall from a man's lips, and I still believe it.

So Mount Moriah will always be held in the highest esteem because of its association with Abraham and Isaac. We all remember that on that mountain God asked a man to do the hardest thing that a man was ever asked to do in this world, and that old hero never even asked God a single question, but got the boy and the wood and the knife and started to the mountain.

We read in Heb. 17:18, 19: "By faith Abraham when he was tried offered up Isaac and he that had received the promise offered up his only begotten son of whom it was said that in Isaac shall thy seed be called, accounting that God was able to raise him up even from the dead from whence also he received him in a figure."

We see that Abraham just as truly killed Isaac and burnt him as if he had done the thing itself, and God gave him credit for killing his son, and so put it down in the sacred Scriptures. So today it stands out that by faith Abraham offered up Isaac, and all men take off their hats to Abraham, and all men take off their hats to Mount Moriah. The very names of Abraham and Mount Moriah are sacred to the Bible reader and the student of sacred history.

In this wonderful tragedy that took place on this mountain we have a beautiful type of God the Father in the man Abraham, and we have a beautiful type of Christ in the boy Isaac, and we have the type of the blessed Holy Ghost in the fire in the hand of Abraham.

We see that Isaac was the child of promise.

Mount Moriah. 15

It had been declared by the Lord Himself that "In Isaac shall all the kindreds of the earth be blessed," and now, right in the face of that promise, God tells Abraham to take Isaac, his only begotten son, and offer him on the altar for a burnt sacrifice. God had just told Abraham that "My covenant will be between me and Isaac.

Now Isaac was not just a common born child; he was the son of a man one hundred years of age, and he was the child of promise. The angels had eaten supper with Abraham and Sarah and promised them this remarkable child. Now according to the word of the angels and according to the promise of the Lord God Himself, this child was born, and is now the joy and comfort of the old father, for he was a wonderful child. But oh, to the sad surprise of Abraham, here comes the voice of God: "Abraham, Abraham!" And he said, "Here I am Lord." And the Lord said to him, "Now take Isaac, thine only son, and get thee to the land that I shall shew thee, and offer up thy son on the altar for a burnt offering." And then just listen! We read that Abraham started. Did he start to leave the country with his boy? Oh no, he started to Mount Moriah to obey God and offer up his son for the burnt offering.

In this wonderful tragedy we see Isaac as a type of the blessed Son of God. Yonder goes Isaac to Mount Moriah with the wood on his shoulder that he is to be burnt on. If you will look down the stream of time a few hundred years you will see the Son of God going to Mount Calvary with the cross of wood on his shoulder, on which He is to die. So without a doubt in my mind, Isaac is the type of Christ.

Just as Isaac was a child of promise, so Christ was the child of promise. He had been promised ever since the fall of man. Now we see God the Father and Abraham each making an offering of their son. Isaac was to bless the whole world of mankind, but the command was to put him to death. Christ was to bless the whole world of mankind, and the command was to put Him to death.

The fire in the hands of Abraham was to consume Isaac, and the Holy Ghost in the hand of the Father is to consume all of the old self that is in us. Just as truly as Abraham received Isaac from the dead, we are to die to this old world, and be put to death and let the fire from heaven fall on us and consume all the dross and tin, and we are to rise and walk in newness of life as new creatures in Christ Jesus. Old things are to pass away, and the Book says, "Behold, all things are new."

Mount Moriah.   17

Abraham just simply believed that God could take the pile of ashes and make his son as truly as he believed that he was on the earth, and so he did not hesitate when God told him to offer up Isaac. Now we can see the force of the statement of Bro. Morrison when he said that "God called and Abraham went, and God promised and Abraham believed, and God asked and Abraham gave."

The reader will remember that it was said of Abraham that he was the "friend of God." It doesn't say that he was friendly with God but it does say that he was the friend of God. There are plenty of people that we are friendly with, but we never tell them anything; but there are others that we tell all we know, and they are the friends, you see. Again, it is said that Abraham is the father of the faithful; again, it is said that Abraham believed God and it was counted unto him for righteousness. I have heard men say, "I would vote the Prohibition ticket, but I am afraid I would lose my vote." Well, the Bible said that, "Abraham believed God and it was counted," and if you will do right God will count you also.

CHAPTER III.

MOUNT HOREB.

Dear reader, we now arrive at the Mount of Fire, or the Mount of Command. Here I see in the Third Chapter of Exodus that God met Moses in the Mount of Horeb, and in the flaming bush the God of heaven spoke to Moses and commanded him to do the greatest thing that a man was ever commanded to do in this world, and not only the greatest, but the hardest thing that a man was ever commanded to do; and that was to go into the land of Egypt and deliver three millions of slaves out of the hand of the greatest nation that was living at that time. And he was to go without gun or buckshot or powder, and not even take a box of caps with him, and yet he was to bring them out with an uplifted hand and with an outstretched arm, and do all this right in the face of the mightiest army on the earth, probably, at that time.

Yonder goes the man to Egypt, and yonder he comes with his people. He must have been successful or he could not have gotten out. But he got out, and as he went he carried the whole nation of his own people with him. Yonder he goes with three millions of slaves, and flocks and herds in abundance, with gold and silver and brass by the donkey loads.

He got his commission from the top of the mountain. When God meets a fellow on the mountain top and tells him something, the fellow never gets over it. And so it is today, the mountain top life is the one altogether lovely, and full of glory and peace and love and joy in the blessed Holy Ghost.

Now there are many things about delivering the Israelites out of Egypt that are very interesting to the Bible student. In the first place, the life of bondage in Egypt is a type of sin, and if a man could be a type of the devil, it was the man Pharaoh, for when the people wanted their freedom then the man Pharaoh set his heart on keeping them in bondage, and in order to keep them there he doubled the task that they already had. How much like the devil that was. How hard the devil makes it on a fellow when he tries to get out of the life of bondage and flee from the life of sin. The devil brings everything in the world to bear on his mind to keep him in bondage.

How natural it is to see them down there in the slime pits gathering straw and making brick under the lash of the taskmasters. Don't you see the poor sinner there, and hear his groan and the lash of the taskmasters? Listen to the command of Pharaoh. He says not one brick shall fail. You must bring up the number of bricks, and if you don't, the lash will be applied.

The poor sinner groans under his burden and the devil laughs at his misery and drives him on. And yet the devil has no right to man's service at all. He is serving the enemy of his soul for nothing, and going to hell and paying the devil to let him go. It looks like they would get their eyes open sometime, but if Moses had not come after them they would have stayed there till they died and never made one effort to escape.

It is true that when Moses got there they did not want him, and so it is today; the people are so blinded by the devil that they don't want the Son of God to reign over them. Nevertheless when they do get their eyes open and see their privileges in Christ Jesus they beat the world to shout and praise God for freedom. Then it will tickle you to death to hear them tell of their burdens as a lost sinner, and then tell how the Lord has saved and sanctified them and delivered them from all sin and made them free and happy in the Lord.

Now as we see the Israelites fleeing from Egyptian bondage, we have before us the sinner fleeing from a life of guilt and condemnation. So the fleeing of the Israelites from a life of bondage is a beautiful type of the convicted sinner fleeing from a life of sin.

But they had not journeyed far till they came to the end of their own strength; they were hedged in between the mountains, and before them rolled the Red Sea, and to their surprise behind them was the rumbling of Pharaoh's chariots and the marching of his mighty army. They cried to Moses who was to them a god, and he told them to stand still and see the salvation of God. He stretched out his rod over the Red Sea and the waters divided and let the Israelites through dry shod.

The reader will notice that the Red Sea is a beautiful type of the Blood of Christ, and when the sinner passes through the Blood by simple faith, he finds the salvation of God. Moses said that is what the Israelites would find— the salvation of God. And Moses said to them that "Today you shall see the Egyptians no more forever." And how true that is to the saved man. If he is true to the Word of the Lord he sees the enemy no more forever, as he has seen him in the days gone by. In the days of the life of sin I saw the devil, my master, and today I see him out there as an enemy, and I have nothing to do with him, and he is not my master any longer, for which I do praise the God of Israel and take courage.

So we see that the crossing of the Red Sea is a beautiful type of conversion. After they had gotten across the Red Sea, we next notice that the Lord gave them manna from heaven, "and it was white, like coriander seed and the taste of it was like waffles made with honey.

But Moses was to lead them on to the land of Canaan; he was to stop with them when he got them out of bondage, but he was to go on to the land of Perfect Love. You will remember that the first sermon he preached after he got to Egypt he told the children of Israel that the land of Canaan was flowing with milk and honey, and he said that it is not like Egypt; it is a land of grapes and olives and pomegranates, and he also said that it was a land of hills and mountains, and springs of water and lands, and houses that you did not build that the Lord will give you.

So we see that Moses got a wonderful commission from the top of the mountain out of the burning bush; no man ever had a greater one than the Lord gave Moses in that remarkable conversation that took place on the mountain that day. I don't wonder that Moses stood and trembled in the sight of that bush and covered his head and dared not behold. I am not surprised that the Lord told him to take the shoes off his feet, for the place on which he stood was holy ground, for the Lord could not commission a man to do as great a thing as Moses was to do and not receive it on hallowed ground. The very mountain was sacred with the presence of God.

No man from that day until now ever received such a commission from either God or man. But the reader will remember that this great commission was delivered to a man on the mountain top. Well, we see by now that the great events of the Bible all took place on the mountain top, which goes to prove to me that the Lord wants us to move upward and onward and outward without a halt or without a let up or a slow up, but with a wagon load of determination to go up and stay up after we get up. Glory to God for the mountain-top of experience!

So we see that Moses was to bring the Israelites out of bondage and across the Red Sea, and give them the manna from heaven, and lead them on to the mountain that we call Mount Sinai, and then he was to give them the Law, and then go up to the land of Canaan. Without a doubt Moses was a second blessing preacher. He was to do more than to get the people converted; he was to take them on to the land of milk and honey, which is not the justified life, but the sanctified life, which every Bible reader knows full well. And I will preach it and sing it and shout it. Glory to God forever and ever. Amen!

CHAPTER IV.

MOUNT SINAI.

Dear reader, we now arrive at the Mount of Honor, or the Mount of Glory, described in the 19th Chapter of the Book of Exodus. I am of the opinion that no mountain has cut as great a swath through history as the mountain that we now have before us, unless it is Mount Calvary, and indeed Mount Sinai and Mount Calvary are twins, for it was at Mount Sinai that God gave the Law, and Mount Calvary is where we receive the Gospel, and on these two hang the hope of man's eternal destiny.

Mount Sinai was on the road between the Red Sea and the Land of Promise. It was at Mt. Sinai that God gave the Law to man, where God spoke to Moses and called him from the plains to the top of the mount, and there descended in a flame of fire and talked to the man Moses face to face forty days and nights, and gave him the Ten Commandments on the tables of stone. For three thousand years men have been trying to bring their lives up to God's beautiful standard:

Thou shalt have no other gods before me.

Thou shalt not make unto thee any graven image, or any likeness of anything that is in heaven above, or that is in the earth beneath, or that is in the water under the earth:

Thou shalt not bow down thyself to them, nor serve them: for I, the Lord thy God, am a jealous God, visiting the iniquity of the fathers upon the children unto the third and fourth generation of them that hate me:

And shewing mercy unto thousands of them that love me, and keep my commandments.

Thou shalt not take the name of the Lord thy God in vain: for the Lord will not hold him guiltless that taketh his name in vain.

Remember the sabbath day, to keep it holy.

Six days shalt thou labor, and do all thy work:

But the seventh day is the sabbath of the Lord thy God: in it thou shalt not do any work, thou, nor thy son, nor thy daughter, thy manservant, nor thy maidservant, nor thy cattle, nor thy stranger that is within the gates:

For in six days the Lord made heaven and earth, the sea, and all that in them is, and rested the seventh day: wherefore the Lord blessed the sabbath day, and hallowed it.

Honor thy father and thy mother: that thy days may be long upon the land which the Lord thy God giveth thee:

Thou shalt not kill.

Thou shalt not commit adultery.

Thou shalt not steal.

Thou shalt not bear false witness against thy neighbor.

Thou shalt not covet thy neighbor's house, thou shalt not covet thy neighbor's wife, nor his manservant, nor his maidservant, nor his ox, nor his ass, nor anything that is thy neighbor's.

It is equal rights of all men to live up to this standard and special rights to none.

The Law was the only man of their counsel

for nearly fifteen hundred years. We see that the first law that God ever gave men was from the top of the Mount Sinai. We see Moses climbing the great old mountain, age-worn and thunder-shaken and lightning-scarred, but on that special occasion we see this holy mount all covered in fire and smoke, and it was made sacred forever on account of the presence of the Almighty God who descended and called Moses up from the congregation of Israelites and talked to him face to face, and then gave the Law and the Commandments to him.

Not only did the Lord then and there give him the Commandments, but the reader will remember that it was on the mountain that God gave Moses the pattern of the tabernacle, which was to be built by him, and from the building of the tabernacle the worship of God took on a new form. Here the Lord was to talk to men from the tabernacle; something new on earth, you see. Up till that time the Lord had used His throne in the sky as a tabernacle to talk to men out of, but after building the temple in the wilderness, we see the Lord coming very near to men and talking to them from between the Cherubims in the little tabernacle. But He gave the pattern to Moses while he was on the mountain.

I am of the opinion that the world has never

seen anything that looked like the mountain on that special occasion. The Israelites at the foot of the mountain fled from the presence of God, and Moses himself said that the sight was so awful that he did exceedingly quake and tremble. It took a man of real courage to climb that mountain, all covered in fire. The glory of the Lord hung over the mountain, and we see from the appearance of Moses when he got back to the camp of Israel that the place must have been something wonderful, for his face shone and the glory to the Lord was on him in such a way that his own brethren could not talk to him, and asked that he put a veil over his face. The beauty of the whole thing was seen in the fact that Moses did not know that the skin of his face shone.

Well, all of that was brought about by Moses keeping company with God on the mountain top. The man that will leave the folks and climb the mountain and meet God will get a shining face every time. No man can keep company with the Lord and not get a little of the presence of the Lord to rub off on himself, and the longer he stays with the Lord the greater the shine. For a man to stand and look at the face of the Lord for forty days he is going to get a glimpse of the Lord to stick to his face. The shining that

Mount Sinai. 31

Moses had was only the reflection of the Lord on the face of Moses.

Mount Sinai made an impression on Moses that he never forgot, and, in fact, never will. He will be telling us about Mount Sinai for the next million years, for it was there he met God face to face, and it was there that God gave him the Law, and it was there that God gave him the Ten Commandments, and it was there God gave him the pattern for the tabernacle and it was there that he tarried forty days and forty nights, as far as we know without eating or drinking and without sleeping. As far as we know, he never got thirsty and never got sleepy and never got tired and never got lonesome or homesick in the least.

So we see that Mount Sinai made an epoch in the life of Moses, such that he will never get over in all time to come. Apart from the presence of God and the burning of the mountain and the giving of the Law there is something about a great mountain that is perfectly beautiful. A man can stand in the presence of a great mountain and feel perfectly awe stricken. A kind of a feeling of greatness and adoration seems to creep over a fellow and he feels like he was in the presence of something that was not man-made. A feeling comes over him that nobody but God can make a mountain. A great mountain will stop the mouth of an infidel and put a padlock on his under jaw, for nobody can make mountains but God. He made Mount Sinai and then He made Moses, and then He gave the Law to Moses from the top of Sinai, and I believe every word of it just the same as if I had been the man that the Lord called to the top of Sinai and given the Law to. I know He did, for the Law is not man-made; it is God-given. It was not gotten up by man; it was handed down from heaven. God Himself was the giver and Moses was the receiver, and we are the keepers and the rejoicers over the fact that God loved this old world well enough to give us a Law and the Commandments.

We are praying and planning and longing to see the day come when we may stand on the top of Mount Sinai and behold His glory with our natural eyes. If it is our Father's will, we want to see the mountain before we go up.

CHAPTER V.

MOUNT NEBO.

Dear reader, we now come to the Mount of Vision, or to Mount Nebo. You remember that Moses in the 34th Chapter of Deuteronomy went from the plains of Moab to the top of Nebo or to Pisgah's heights to view the Promised Land before he went to live with the Lord. We see him standing on the top of Nebo and God seemed to touch his eyes and he was permitted to see the land from Gilead to Dan, but was not allowed to go over and take possession of the goodly land that he had been working for for the past eighty years. No doubt he thought that God would send him with the people out of bondage forty years before He sent him to do it, and now after at least forty years of as hard trials as a man ever went through in this world, Moses is allowed to go to the mountain top and view the Land of Promise.

There he was to die and his funeral was to be held, and there was to be nobody there but the Lord himself. The funeral of the man Moses was too sacred to be held by mortal man, and again, the Lord knew that if He let the world know where the grave of Moses was that, not only the Israelites, but the world would almost worship the grave of Moses. Well, I will leave out the word "almost." I suppose that if I knew just where the grave of Moses was that I would be willing to almost pay any kind of a price to get to see the grave of Moses, and we would see thousands of men that never keep the Law of Moses that would cross the oceans to see the grave of the man Moses.

We see the old hero in the last conversation with his children, for the Old Book says that for forty years he carried them as a mother carried her children in her bosom, so we see that he was a mother to them as well as a father, and he was to them as a god. Now the time comes for the separation, and the Lord speaks to him and tells him to get himself up out of the plains of Moab to the top of Nebo. We find that the last conversation that ever took place between Moses and the children of Israel is recorded in the 33rd Chapter of the Book of Deuteronomy. In the opening of the 34th Chapter we see him on the way to the mountain. What wonderful experiences the man Moses had on the tops of Mountains. He got his commission to go to Egypt and deliver

Israel, from the top of Mount Horeb, and he went and did the greatest work that was ever done by any living man; and he got the call from the Lord while he was in the plains to come to the top of Mount Sinai and receive the Law, and he went and received it, and we have it today. Now, as he finishes up his life's work the Lord has him to come to the top of Nebo to die.

What a great thing it was to get to die on the top of a beautiful mountain. He was just out of the sight of the Israelites when he died, but he was in sight of the land of Canaan and in sight of heaven and in the presence of God. If ever the angels did want to see what was going on, it was while the Lord was burying the body of Moses, for I tell you, my friend, three worlds were interested while the Lord buried Moses. I have not heard of all the funerals of the earth, but I am of the opinion that there was never another funeral just like the one we have before us. If ever a man in this world was buried in great pomp and glory, it was the man Moses. How in the world could anything be greater than his funeral? The idea of the Lord Himself coming down to this earth and burying a man and holding the funeral Himself!

Brother, I have seen men with black crape

on their arms and other men with big hats with plumes on them, and the horses all draped in mourning, and the men with their little white aprons on, and white gloves on, walk around the grave and throw in a shovel full of dirt and say, "Alas, my brother!" but when you think of the funeral of Moses, their little show makes a fellow sick. Of course, that is the best they can do, and I am not finding fault with them, I am only stating a fact.

The reader will remember that the title that Moses wore was this: "Moses, the servant of God." Now that was his title. He was not an A. M., or a D. D., or an LL.D., or a Ph. D., and they never called him Dr., but notice his title, "Moses, the servant of the Lord." No wonder he had a mountain to die on. No wonder he was commissioned from the top of a mountain. No wonder he received the Law from the top of a mountain. No wonder he had the privilege of going to the top of Nebo to die. No wonder he had a funeral unlike any other that is left on record. No wonder he had the Lord God of the whole earth to bury him, for his title is unlike anybody's I ever heard of; just simply "The servant of the Lord." The title he wore cut him off from the people; he was not the people's man, he was the Lord's man, and of course when the time came for him to die, it was the Lord's place to look after him, and thank the Lord He did it, and the world has never quit talking about it.

Hundreds of years after the burying was over, we hear the devil raising a racket about the body of Moses, but the angels paid no attention at all. The thing did not concern the devil, for the Bible says that "Moses was the servant of the Lord." But how different it would have been if Moses had been the servant of the devil. He never would have seen the Land of Canaan from the top of Mount Nebo, but thank the Lord he did just the same. The Lord knows His own, and the Lord knew that Moses was His man, and the devil had no claim on Moses at all.

The reader will remember that the devil is a mightier man for tombstones, and the thing that he wanted was a tall spire to go at the head of the grave of Moses, but the Lord knew that a man with the record that Moses had did not need a tombstone, for they represent the dead, and Moses is still alive. Glory to God in the highest!

CHAPTER VI.

MOUNT HEBRON.

The Mount of Possession. Dear reader, we read in the 14th Chapter of the Book of Joshua, that when Caleb was four score and five years old he said to Joshua, "Give me this mountain for a possession forever," and we read that Joshua blessed him and gave him the mountain for an everlasting possession.

One beautiful thing about it is that when he got in possession of this wonderful gift it was on his birthday, the day that he was 85 years old. Another thing that I want you to notice is the kind of gift that this man asked for. He surely had lofty desires; he asked for a mountain. That was the biggest thing in the world. He did not ask for a mole hill, and he did not ask for a beautiful plain; he wanted to get possession of the thing that could be seen from a distance.

A plain is beautiful, but you cannot see it if you are not down on it; and the little hills are beautiful, but you can't see them very far; but when you look at that great old mountain lifting its head above all the country for hundreds of miles around, you are made to stand bewildered and you feel like taking off your hat and bowing down to that great mountain. I am not surprised when I hear of the poor heathen worshipping the great mountains of their nation. When I stood yonder at the foot of Pike's Peak in the great old Rockies, a feeling of love and a feeling of admiration stole over me. As I stood and gazed at that mountain with his old head all covered with snow and the top of his head three miles above the level of the sea, I said, "Nobody but the God that I love and worship could make anything that looks like that."

So we see the greatness of the man's character when we see his choice. It is just so today. You see some men that make a choice and it is tobacco, and others make a choice and it is liquor, and others make a choice and it is hogs, and others make a choice and it is cows, and still others make a choice and it is horses, and others too numerous to mention, make all kinds of choices that go to make up the real character of the man. It has been said, "Show me the kind of a book a man reads and I will tell you what kind of a man he is." It could be just as truly said, "Tell me what kind of a choice the man made and I will give you the man's character."

Mount Hebron.   41

You can see the greatness of Caleb's when you see his choice. He said, "Give me Mount Hebron," and there the old hero sits on the side of that great old mountain with a sparkling, splashing spring bursting from the mountain side to sing Caleb to sleep at night. He said that he got that gift because he wholly followed the Lord. Now beloved, if a man can follow the Lord in such a way as to get possession of a mountain don't you think that it is worth his time and his energy to seek and strive for it? I get the lesson that we are to have a mountain-top experience.

If Caleb could get a mountain by wholly following the Lord, if you and I would wholly follow the Lord He would give us a mountain also. The Book says that there is no respect of persons with Him, and if that is so, and we know it is, we can have as much as Caleb. He got Mount Hebron, not to keep till the camp meeting was over, but for an *everlasting* possession.

There is something about the religion of Jesus Christ that is elevating and uplifting. You may see a man one week all dirty and ragged, and you may let that same man get a good case of old fashioned, heart-felt religion, the next week you will see the same man all cleaned up and washed and with clean clothes on. His clothes may be ragged, but he will wash them, and you will see a great change in the man. In only one week he will look like a bran new man, and if you did not know that he was the same fellow you would not believe your own eyes. I have seen men one week look like a beast, and the next week they would look like a man, and by the next week look like a gentleman, and by the next week would look like a saint. Well, what ailed him? Well, you can see that he has got rid of sin, and the reforming grace of God has come into that man's heart and life, and he is a new creature and old things have passed away and behold all things have become new. You are not looking at the man that you saw last week. The old man that you saw last week is dead and his funeral has been preached and the last song has been sung over the last sin that he ever committed. He is a delivered man and is now ready to climb the mountain.

If it were preached to the young converts all over the country, and if all the people of God expected them to get the experience of sanctification, they would like to go to the mountain top at once and think nothing of it. But the devil on the outside and the preachers on the inside have made the people believe

Mount Hebron. 43

that they could not live a holy life, and they have settled down to the life of plains and swamps and mud holes and hollows and valleys.

Off yonder in the distance is the great old Mount Hebron, and old Caleb said to Joshua, "Give me this mountain." Caleb had no thought of living down in the valley. Well, I don't blame him at all, do you? If it was to do over again I would shout while Caleb climbed the mountain side. It is perfectly natural to hear the holiness people sing all over the United States, "I am dwelling on the mountain, where the golden sunlight gleams," and then you will hear them sing, "I can see far down the mountain where I wandered weary years, often hindered in my journey by the ghost of doubts and fears." Then notice again, "Broken vows and disappointments thickly sprinkled all the way." Now I don't remember the author of that old hymn, but his theology is as true as the rising and the setting of the sun. Thank the Lord for the good example we have before us. Just listen: "Give me this mountain for an everlasting possession." Now children, do we want the mountain-top experience? If so, let's go and possess the Land.

CHAPTER VII.

MOUNT CARMEL.

The Mount of Contest, or the Mount of Victory for God's folks, and the Mount of Defeat for the devil's crowd. Well, dear reader, we have now to come to Mount Carmel, the battle ground of Elijah, where he met eight hundred and fifty false prophets of Baal in the grove. Here one man met not only a king and queen, eight hundred and fifty backslidden preachers, but a whole nation of God-forgetters, and defeated the whole crowd.

There was a hostile king and queen backed up by eight hundred and fifty preachers who seemed to hate the very ground Elijah walked on. They had scoured the woods and hills and mountains and the caves; the holes of the earth had been searched for this man, and they had sworn eternal vengeance against him if they could find him, for "he was the troubler of Israel." But bless God, right in the midst of their hostility the old hero appeared on the scene and challenged King Ahab to gather all Israel together on Mount Carmel, and with all Israel together, the four hundred and fifty prophets of Baal and also four hundred prophets of the grove, and they would have a special meeting and prove their gods and see who was right and who was wrong.

Of course they had to accept the challenge, and now it is up to them to meet the old hairy man, as they called him, and prove the great god, that they called Baal. The king had accepted the challenge. The false prophets all claimed that Baal was a god, and the people did not know but what he was. The old prophet Elijah said that Baal was no god and no good, and that all Israel was under a delusion of the devil, and when he talked in that way the servants of Baal all boiled over and sorry to say, they are still boiling.

And now, right in the face of the greatest annual conference that ever met in Palestine, this old holiness man came to the conference and put all the preachers to one of the straightest tests that was ever put to a set of men, and it was put in such a way that they had to accept it. It was this: "The God that answers by fire, let him be God; if it is Baal or if it is the God of Israel, the one that answers by fire, he is to be God. And all the people said, It is well spoken." Of course they were deceived by the prophets of Baal, and without doubt they thought that Baal's preachers would be

Mount Carmel. 47

able to get the fire and defeat the old hairy man who had given them so much trouble. He preached holiness and the other crowd preached worldliness, and the folks did not want holiness and they did not want worldliness, but they had something else before sundown.

"Now," said Elijah, "you are many and I will give you the first test. Now go to work and build you an altar and put your wood on it and then slay your bullock and lay him on the wood and put no fire on it or under it, and you call on your god and if he sends fire and consumes the bullock, Baal is to be the god. I will build an altar and put the wood on it and I will slay the bullock and put him on the wood and put no fire under it and I will call on the God of Israel, and the God that answers by fire he is to be the God." Now the test is on, and the king is to watch the proceedings; and not only the king, but the whole nation was watching with bated breath to see how the thing would come out.

It is to be the God of Israel, or it is to be Baal, one or the other. Never did a man-made god have any better chance than Baal had that day. And if Baal could not do something on that great occasion he was a flat failure, for they were there from all over the country, and eight hundred and fifty of Baal's strongest men were there. They were there from Vanderbilt and from Harvard and from Yale and from Columbia and from Stanford. All of their own nation, and several from abroad representing Oxford and Berlin and Edinburgh. The pomp and glory of Baal never shone so bright as on that great occasion.

One little, old man covered with a camel-skin cloak sat down to see the display of Baal and to see the religious worship. Of course Baal never did anything on a small scale. The king and queen and their eight hundred and fifty Doctors of Divinity with a nation at their command made one of the most interesting crowds that a holiness man ever faced. The only thing that saved him was the fact that he had the blessing, and no make believe about it. If he had been the least bit shaky they would have backed him out. But oh my beloved! he never even looked down his nose one time. He sat by in an humble attitude, but it was not because he feared Baal, for he knew that he fought a winning battle. He watched them as the religious performance went on. They had no idea on earth that one man was more than a match for eight hundred and fifty. The eight hundred and fifty had everything on their side,

Mount Carmel. 49

but One, and that saved Elijah, for that One was God. They had the world and the flesh and the devil in as great pomp as you ever put your two eyes on, but the thing that they did not have was the very thing that Elijah did have, and that was the God of Israel. Amen.

The thing is beginning to get interesting about this time of day, and the prayers are long and loud and many, and they are coming thick and fast. They are up against an awful proposition ,and it is, "O Baal, hear us! O Baal, it will never do for you to go back on us at this trying time. Just look yonder at that old hairy man with a smile all over his face. He is now making fun of us and what will he do, Baal, if you don't send fire? O Baal, you must send the fire. The time will soon be over for our test and the fire has not come yet, and we don't feel right about it some how. We are a little bit uneasy, and this old man is watching us, and he seems to be perfectly contented. Anl now Baal, if ever you did send fire you must send it now." And if Baal could have said a word, he would have whispered to them and said, "I never did send fire, and never will, for when you made me you left out the qualities that produce fire, that is life. No fire without life." And as Baal was man-made he did not propose to send fire.

The thing got so ridiculous that at noon Elijah mocked them and said, "Baal is surely a god; he must be asleep or he may be perusing, or peradventure he is in a conversation and you must do something to attract him." And then they went for Baal in a most marvelous way. They drew their knives and cut themselves and leaped up and down on their altars and cried, "O Baal, hear us!" But the Bible says that there was none to regard or to hear what was going on on the holy mount called Carmel.

But the time came for the evening sacrifice, and the man of God called all the people near to him, and we read that he repaired the altar of the Lord that had been thrown down. And he took twelve stones to represent the twelve tribes of Israel, and he built the altar to the Lord. He hewed his wood and put it on the altar and then he slayed his bullock and laid him in order, and then he went to work and had them dig a trench around the altar that would hold twelve barrels of water, and he had them pour twelve barrels of water over the sacrifice, and soak it with water. Now these false prophets knew that water would put out fire, and the old prophet was not going to leave them one excuse to hide behind.

If he had not put on the water they would have said that he had the fire hid under the wood somewhere, but they all saw the sacrifice soaked in water, and now while they look on, the old servant of the Lord drops down on his knees and offers up a short prayer to the God of Israel, and to their surprise the fire fell, and all the people shouted, "The Lord, he is God! the Lord, he is God!"

Now the test is over, and Elijah's God won out in the contest, and the old prophet had these eight hundred and fifty false prophets put to death, for they were impostors and deceivers.

CHAPTER VIII.

MOUNT OF TEMPTATION.

Dear reader, we have now arrived at the first mountain experience that is recorded in the New Testament, and it is found in the Fourth Chapter of St. Matthew's Gospel. It is the record of the awful temptation of the blessed Son of God, and it might properly be called the Mount of Temptation, or we might call it the Mount of Victory for the Son of God, and the Mount of Defeat for the devil. Just as truly as the devil defeated King Saul on Mount Gilboa, the Son of God defeated the devil on this mountain and came off more than Conqueror, and won the battle for us, and today we have to make war with a devil that has been defeated by our Christ. We are better able to meet his onslaughts by the fact that the Son of God met him in the open field and defeated him and came out more than a Victor.

The devil knows that Christ is on our side, and he knows that the blessed Christ has defeated him, and that we know it as well as he does. And he knows that we are fighting a winning battle, for the war is between Christ and the devil, and the devil knows just as well as he knows anything that Christ is to run him down and put him off this planet and set up His Kingdom in this world and reign from shore to shore. We read that the devil has come down to this earth with great wrath because he knows that his time is short. Of course we think that a few years of suffering and toil and temptation from the devil is a very long time, but the few years that we are on probation are as nothing compared to the eternities that are to unfold and pass on by. And today we can see that victory is ours in the end, and that is the thing that keeps us in good courage.

We know that the devil is fighting a losing battle while we are fighting a winning battle, but while the devil knows that he is defeated, he is not going to give you up without an awful struggle on his part to keep you in his kingdom of darkness and death, and hell at last. He has defeated many a soul since Jesus won the battle for them. The devil made them believe that they were not free, and that he had a perfect right to them and their service and their money and their influence. How many poor souls he has put into hell is unknown by us, and yet every one of

Mount of Temptation.   55

them had been redeemed by the blessed Son of God, and a way opened up whereby they every one could escape the snares of the devil and make their way to heaven.

Jesus fought out this awful battle on the Mount of Temptation, and then on the cross He bought us and paid for us with His own precious blood, and today we are His by creation and redemption and preservation. And I am His by my own choice, and my own free will power, bless His holy name.

The Christian who knows nothing of temptation that stands out in his life like a mountain, has not been long in the way, for the devil has a wilderness to take every fellow through, and a mountain-like temptation that will stand just before you. The Lord will permit the devil to give to you this test because He wants a people that He has tried and proven, and the one way the Lord has of trying us is to turn the devil loose on us, and what he will do to us will be a plenty. The Lord will give us grace to come out victorious, and then we have one more defeat recorded over the devil and one more victory recorded for our blessed Savior, and we sing, "Each victory will help you some other to win," and nobody knows that any better than the fellow who has been through the battle.

We all know that it is one thing to write about the temptation, and one thing to sing about it, but to be sorely tried by the devil is altogether another thing. I am willing to admit that at times I have been so sorely tried, it looked to me that I would die under temptation. When I have been most sorely tried was not when the devil was tempting me to do something that was wrong; he has tried me on all of those things, but the most awful trials that I have ever had from the devil were when he would swoop down on me and seemed to close up every avenue of prayer and every avenue of faith and hope, and the arm of trust seemed to be broken, and the awful darkness would settle down over me, and my soul was tossed as a vessel out on the bosom of the great deep. Then it seemed that all the powers of hell were turned loose on me at one time, and there was nothing to do but just stand still and see the salvation of the Lord. While these temptations were going on, there was no temptation to do anything, either good or bad. Our trials will cause us to remember the words of St. Peter when he said that "The trying of your faith is more precious than gold."

CHAPTER IX.

THE MOUNT OE BLESSING.

We have now come to what is one of the most interesting mountains described in the Holy Bible, the Mount of Blessings or the Mount of the Beatitudes. Here was given the "Sermon on the Mount." We have gotten used to talking about the Sermon on the Mount, and we have, in our use of them, connected together the two words "sermon" and "mount" until we can't separate them. They are joined together, and we say what God hath joined together, let no man put asunder.

Just why the Son of God went to the top of a mountain to preach this, the most wonderful discourse the world ever heard or ever will hear, is not as easy to explain as it is to ask. We might ask why did he go to the top of this mountain to preach this wonderful sermon and you probably could not answer the question. Why He did it I don't know, but we know that He did. It seems that mountains had a wonderful fascination for the Son of God. He could be found out on the mountain top most any time.

We find in the Sermon on the Mount more than one hundred verses, and we have heard it said by men who study the subjects of the Bible very closely, that He discussed one great subject in each verse. In this wonderful discourse there is nothing common to man, but what he discussed thoroughly. He opens this wonderful sermon with nine blessings such as were new to the world. Notice them: Blessed are the poor in spirit; blessed are they that mourn; blessed are the meek; blessed are they that do hunger and thirst after righteousness; blessed are the merciful; blessed are the pure in heart; blessed are the peacemakers; blessed are they who are persecuted for righteousness' sake; blessed are you when men shall revile you.

Then He takes up this thought and says to the Christian, "Ye are the salt of the earth." One is a healing, cleansing, purifying power, and the other is a life-giving energy. Nothing gives life like light, and nothing protects life like salt. He teaches how to pray, and He teaches how to fast, and He teaches how to give, and He teaches how to love, and He teaches how to worship. In fact, anything that you want to know is explained in the Sermon on the Mount. And when we say that all Christian doctrine is founded on the teachings of the Sermon on the Mount, we do not overdraw the statement, for there is no way to have a religious creed in the land of Bibles without taking into it the Sermon on the Mount. I suppose that millions of sermons have been preached from this one great sermon, and today there is plenty of it left for the whole human family and to spare.

In this remarkable sermon we have what is known as the Lord's Prayer, and it is unlike anything else on the whole earth. Nobody ever got up anything that looks or reads like the Lord's Prayer. I suppose that every Sunday morning many millions of Christians repeat the Lord's Prayer. But while we call it the Lord's Prayer, we all know that it is our prayer, for He said, "When you pray, pray after this manner:" And then He proceeded to word for us what we call the Lord's Prayer.

Again, we see another prayer dictated to us by Him in this remarkable Sermon. He said to us, "Ask and it shall be given you," then He said, "Seek and ye shall find, and knock and it shall be opened unto you." Then listen to the next words He uttered: "For every one that asketh receiveth and he that seeketh findeth, and to him that knocketh it shall be opened." There is no room for doubt. He said, ye shall find, and I believe it with all my heart, don't you?

I am of the opinion that the world has never been the same since the day that Christ preached the Sermon on the Mount. At one time he said, "The words that I speak unto thee, they are spirit and they are life," and when we read the Sermon on the Mount we know that He meant just what He said. The words uttered by Him on that great occasion were the words of life. How the infidel and skeptic and agnostic and the higher critic and unbelievers are to be pitied by the man that knows God the Father and God the Son and the Holy Ghost! The man who has sat down and read with pleasure the Sermon on the Mount and believes it, has nothing to fear from the unbeliever and the skeptics, for he can sing with Brother John T. Benson, of Nashville, Tenn.:

> My feet have found the resting place,
> I am on the Rock at last, at last;
> My feet have found the resting place,
> I am on the Rock at last.

Will Huff would say that the man who has the Sermon on the Mount in his heart has something that is rock-ribbed to stand on.

Amen and Amen!

CHAPTER X.

MOUNT OF TRANSFIGURATION.

Dear reader, we have now arrived at the foot of another great mountain with a remarkable history. We see this mountain recorded in the 17th Chapter of St. Matthew's Gospel, and it is called the Mount of Transfiguration. On this mountain we have a wonderfully interesting piece of history. The disciples had been with Jesus almost three years and had only seen Him as a man. But on the mount they saw Him in His glorified body. We read that His face did shine as the sun and His raiment was as white as the light. And then we read, "And behold there appeared unto them Moses and Elias talking with him;" and we turn back and notice that it had been 1451 years since Moses had his funeral on the mountain top across the river Jordan from the promised land. After the death of Moses we hear nothing more of him for 1451 years, but to our surprise here he is on the Mount of Transfiguration. We look at the other fellow who is on the mount and behold it is Elijah, and he had been gone 896 years.

So we have before us the Law-giver and the prophet and the Savior. The Savior had said that he would not pass away until all the Law and the Prophets were fulfilled, and now here on this mountain we have in the presence of three witnesses: Peter, James and John, the Christ of the Old and New Testaments. Now here stands before us the man that gave the Law to the world, and we have before us the greatest Prophet that ever lived. No other man ever did such things as Elijah. The prayer that brought the three years famine and the prayer that brought the rain, and the prayer that brought the fire from heaven, and the slaying of eight hundred and fifty false prophets.

When we read that Peter wanted to build three houses and live on the mountain top we are not surprised, for today if we were to get into the presence of the Son of God, and if Moses and Elias were to appear on the scene, we would want to stay there and ask questions about our loved ones.

In this wonderful scene on the mountain top we have three great proofs before us, and they are as follows: We have Moses there to represent all the dead, and he proves the resurrection. In the case of Moses we see that the dead will be resurrected and will stand at the

Judgment Bar of God as natural as if they had never died. We see this proven by Moses, for here is a man that had been dead 1451 years, and we see him as natural as if he had never died. So Moses in the Mount of Transfiguration represents all the dead in Christ. We remember that Elijah never died but was translated, and went up without ever tasting death, but there he stands on the mountain top as natural as if he had just come from Mt. Carmel. In this wonderful transfiguration we see that Elijah represents all the living, for he never died, but we see him as natural as he ever was in this life. He never became an angel while he was gone. He still remained the old Prophet, and the very moment that Peter flashed his eyes on him he knew him and called him by name. So that proves that we will know each other in the Land so fair. Some people have always had their doubts as to whether we will know each other in heaven or not. Well, we need have no more trouble about that. We surely will have as much sense in heaven as we have on earth. We know our loved ones here and of course we will know them there.

Another fact that we have brought out on the Mount of Transfiguration is that we have settled forever who is to be our leader. While the face of the Lord was shining like the sun, we hear the voice of the Father saying, "This is my well beloved Son, hear him." Notice He did not say to hear Moses, or to hear Elijah, but He said "hear him," that is, hear Christ. While we are to honor all men to whom honor is due, we are to hear the Son of God and we are to obey Him and Him only.

The preacher of the gospel is to hear the Son of God anl get his message from Him, and they are to be fresh from heaven; not man-made, but heaven-born; not to be reasoned out, but they are to be revealed from heaven to the God-made preacher and not the school-made man. The schools may help a man a little, but if a man only has what the schools can give him he is to be pitied, for the poorest preachers on the face of the earth are men who are just out of school full of self and ignorant of God, and as empty as a tin horn, with no knowledge of God or of the blessed Holy Ghost. I am sure the Lord would use a man with good education if He could get him, but the trouble is this: when a man goes a few years to the schools and finds out enough to make him useful, the devil jumps on the poor fellow with both feet and stamps him into the ground, and makes him believe that he is too

Mount of Transfiguration. 65

important to give his useful life to the Church of the Lord Jesus, and the thing for him to do is to go into the things of the world: Law or Medicine, or the stage. Most anything will beat being a preacher.

And so the devil catches the most of the men out of the schools, but the Lord in His divine providence just takes boys and girls out of the corn fields or from the cook stove or the wash tub and converts them and then sanctifies them and fills them with the Holy Ghost and puts them out on exhibition for the world to look at. He gives them mounts of transfiguration and reveals Himself to them, and the Scriptures all open up to such a fellow and he lives in and revels in the Holy Bible. He has mounts of holy worship, and mountains of low, and mountains of vision and mountains of possession, then mountains of contest, and mountains of temptation, and mountains of blessings, and then his mount of choice, and at last his mount of transfiguration, where he will know Moses as the lawgiver, and Elijah as the great prophet, and, thank God! he will know the Son of God as his Leader, and his Guide, and his Protector, and his Keeper, and his all and in all. He will be a living, walking example of what God can do for a man in this old world, and he will live the mountain-top life which is nothing more or less than the blessing of holiness as a second work of grace, received by faith subsequent to regeneration.

The mountain-top life is the one, and don't you stop short of it, beloved; don't you listen to the devil any longer, but press your claim to the throne of grace and tell your heavenly Father that you have come after a mountain, and that you will not be satisfied with a mole hill, or a big ridge; nothing short of a mountain will satisfy you in this world. Well, glory to God! Amen!

CHAPTER XI.

MOUNT CALVARY.

We have now come to Mount Calvary, which is the hope of this world. We read in the four Gospels, Matthew, Mark, Luke and John, of the crucifixion of the blessed Son of God. Of course all the mountains are very interesting, and something wonderful has taken place on them all, but the thing that is worth most to this lost world is the thought that the blessed Christ was crucified on the mountain top for the redemption of this world.

The hope of heaven hangs on the Mount of Calvary. The hope of heaven is seen there; the hope of the poor sinner is there, and the hope of the believer is there. The songs that have stirred the world have been songs that were written in the blood of the blessed Son of God. He had to die to shed His blood, and He died on the top of Mount Calvary, so we have to look in that direction to see salvation, or heaven, or hope, or light, or life, or anything that lifts and elevates man and puts him at his best for God and the world, with its suffering humanity.

We all look from the beautiful church with its hard-wood pews and Brussels carpets and thundering organ and red-wood pulpit, to the cross of Christ on the mountain.

We read that without the shedding of blood there is no remission, and back behind the shedding of the blood is the cross, and the cross stood on Mount Calvary. Just why the Son of God went to Calvary to die I don't know, but we know that he did, and that is enough for us to know. We never will get out of reach of Calvary. There is no sin that is known to the human family, outside of the sin against the Holy Ghost, but there is power enough at Mount Calvary to blot out. All the sins of the universe have been piled on the Son of God at Calvary and He bore them all away. I used to think that there, on that great occasion, He made atonement for all the sins that had ever been committed, but it covered more ground than that, for it had to reach forward to all the sins that ever would be committed, and make a provision for them all.

About 1900 years after the blessed Christ hung on the cross of Calvary, I was born and went into a life of sin. At the age of twenty-one I heard of the death of the blessed Christ for the remission of my sins, and I wept my way to the altar, and repented of my sins, and confessed my sins, and forsook my sins, and believed on the blessed Son of God. And from Calvary there came out pardon, full and free, and the blood-stained cross stood out before me and I saw that there was hope for the guilty sinner. My faith took hold of the shed blood, the light of heaven broke in on my poor lost soul, and I got up out of the straw with the shine on my face, and the glory in my soul. From that day until this I have had springs in my heels and a well in my soul and the glory in my eye and a hope that reached away beyond the grave and out into the eternities. Well, glory to God! it is enough to make a fellow shout just to talk about it.

So we go up and down in this old world singing such songs as

"At the cross, at the cross where I first saw the light,
And the burden of my heart rolled away."

And somebody else will take up the chorus and begin to sing

"Calvary's stream is flowing."

And somebody else will take up another old hymn and begin to sing

"It was there on its side He suffered and died
To redeem a poor sinner like me."

We have found out that a religion that has no cross in it and no Calvary in it and no blood in it is a dead religion, and a hopeless religion. A lifeless religion is man-made and dies with its creator, which is man.

The Apostle Paul, the greatest preacher that the world ever saw, said, "God forbid that I should glory save in the cross of our Lord Jesus Christ, by whom the world is crucified unto me and I unto the world." The Apostle was dead to the world, and the world was dead to him. He did not want anything that belonged to the world, and the world did not want anything that belonged to him. Calvary means death to the world. It is a disgrace to the cause of Christ to hear church members, who trot to the theatre and card table and ball room, talk of a crucifixion. To my mind it a real sport for the devil. In the name of the Christ Who shed His blood on Moust Calvary, how can they dare to stand in the presence of God and talk about being crucified when there is nothing they are dead to but scriptural salvation? They are as much alive to the works of the devil as he himself is, and they are as dead to the works of the Church as the devil. In many places these people are the leaders in the house of God. I don't wonder that the Son of God said upon one occasion that the "harlots go into the kingdom of heaven before you." When He spoke those awful words He was talking to the elders and chief priests, at that time the rulers of the house of God.

The latest thing that comes to my hearing is in one of the little cities out in Ohio. There, in the First Methodist Church, is a young lady who sings in the choir on Sunday morning. While I was in the town holding a revival there was a big ball in the city, and the girl danced with the devil. They had the thing all arranged, and she was dressed for the great occasion, and of course the devil was all arranged to act his part. The lights were turned low, or turned out, I don't know which, and the devil came in and this young lady danced with the devil. Of course she knew the devil; he was a young man in the city whom she kept company with and he a sinner. A sinner keeping company with a woman who passed herself for a Christian, and in the ball room dancing with a man who is supposed to be the devil! What faith could he have in the religion of that young woman? She is as sure to put him in the pit of despair as the world stands, if he is led by her influence. Wouldn't she be a pretty spectacle up in the choir next Sunday morning? Just think of a woman in the choir on Sunday morning, and in the arms of the devil on Tuesday night.

There is no Mount Calvary there; there is no pleading for the lost there; there is no life hid with Christ in God there; there is no witness of the Spirit there; there is no baptism with the Holy Ghost there. Just listen to a few words from the Methodist discipline: "Dost thou renounce the devil and all his works, and the vain pomp and glory of the world, with all covetous desires of the same, so that thou shalt not follow or be led by them?" And she said, "I renounce them all."

Well, there is but one hope, and that is to keep our eyes on Mount Calvary and press our claims to the gates of the devil for a devil that can degrade the women of the earth and leave them hopeless and in dark despair, and come into a Christian nation and into the Methodist Church and drag the women of America down on his level, is a pretty shrewd devil. We had better sing

> "The cleansing stream, I see, I see,
> I plunge and oh it cleanseth me."

Amen and Amen.

CHAPTER XII.

MOUNT OF COMMISSION.

We have now come to the Mount of Commission, or the blessed Son of God sending out the disciples from the top of one of the mountains of Galilee. We read in St. Matt. 18: 16, 19, 20: "Go ye therefore and teach all nations baptizing them in the name of the Father and of the Son and of the Holy Ghost, teaching them to observe all things whatsoever I have commanded you, and lo, I am with you alway even unto the end of the world." Here the blessed Son of God gave the greatest commission that was ever given to a set of men in this world. Just listen to the commission: "Go ye therefore and teach all nations," and then what? "Baptizing them in the name of the Father and in the name of the Son and in the name of the Holy Ghost." And then He puts in another clause and says, "Teaching them to observe all things whatsoever I have commanded you," and then listen, "Lo, I am with you alway even unto the end of the world."

The reader will notice that the disciples got

their commission from the top of a mountain, and not the bottom of the valley, or even from the banks of a beautiful spring branch. How wonderful it seems to me to think that the blessed Christ went to the top of a mountain to do all of His wonderful works. We see Him on the mountain when He is undergoing his awful temptation; we see Him on the mountain when He preached that sermon that every man and woman and child loves to read; and we see Him on the mountain when he makes His choice and calls His twelve Apostles; and we see Him on the mount when He was glorified and "his face did shine as the sun and his raiment was as white as the light;" and He went on the mountain to be crucified; and now we see Him on the mountain when He is giving His disciples the greatest commission that a set of men ever received in this world.

Oh, the wonderful things that God has told His children on mountains. What scenes have taken place around and near by and on the top of the mountains of the earth. How the Son of God loved to hang around the mountains. His preaching and His praying was mostly done on the mountains of Judea.

After the parting words of the Master, the disciples went down from the top of that

Mount of Commission. 75

mountain to do a work that they never would have done without the great commission from the Master on the mount of victory and glory and honor and power and love, for all this hung over the mountain while the Christ was giving these men this wonderful commission. There was so much included. It was to change the whole world. The lives and customs and work of men were to be changed by the commission to these Galilean fishers who had traveled with the blessed Son of God for three years. Not only did this great commission reach out and affect the whole world, but it meant that the men who received this wonderful commission were to preach a new doctrine to the world; and not only that, but they were to seal their doctrine by their blood. Their commission meant not only to preach, but to perish by the sword; not only dig for their bread, but die for their cause; and as far as we know not one of them escaped. Their lives were taken, their heads were severed from their bodies, but they stood so true that today the people of the earth are naming their children for them and naming their churches for them.

But back behind all is the Mount of Crucifixion, and the Mount of Commission. On one of these mountains the disciples saw their

Lord and Master die; and on the other mountain they heard the same Master say, "Go into all the world and preach the gospel to every creature, and he that believeth and is baptized shall be saved, and he that believeth not shall be damned." Their commission stayed with them until the day of their death. I suppose that if the Lord ever calls a man to preach, that he will never lose his commission to preach the message of the Lord. I have seen men that I am sure had been called to preach the gospel, and had backslidden, and I verily believe that while they were in their backslidden state the call to preach was still with them and they felt it as much as ever. While they were down in the life of sin, while the devil was beating and cuffing them they could hear the voice of the Master calling them to the field of labor, and at times their hearts would burn within them and they would feel like going back to the work again. I have heard men preach while they themselves were down, and the Lord would bless the message to my own soul. He would honor His Word and make it a blessing to multitudes of people. That is the reason that men can have revivals after they have backslidden. They still have the commission from the Master, "Go ye."

CHAPTER XIII.

MOUNT OLIVET.

Dear reader, we have now come to the Mount of Ascension, or the Son of God ascending to the right hand of the Father. We read that while He yet talked to them He was taken up out of their sight into heaven. We read in Acts 1:9-12: "And when he had spoken these things while they beheld he was taken up and a cloud received him out of their sight; and while they looked steadfastly toward heaven as he went up, behold two men stood by them in white apparel, which also said, Ye men of Galilee, why stand ye gazing up into heaven? This same Jesus which is taken up from you into heaven shall so come in like manner as ye have seen him go into heaven. Then returned they into Jerusalem from the Mount called Olivet, which is from Jerusalem a Sabbath day's journey."

The beauty of this mountain is this that the feet of the blessed Son of God stood on Mount Olivet up to the last minute that He stood on the earth. The last tracks that Jesus ever made were on Mount Olivet. When He left

Olivet He went back to the right hand of the Father. He had been in this country for more than thirty years on a mission that meant everything on earth to us, for it was the plan or scheme of human redemption. He had conquered the world and the flesh and the devil, and had redeemed us and bought us with His blood. Now He is ready to leave this world and go back to the right hand of the Father. He led the disciples out to Mount Olivet and lifted up His hands and blessed them, and while he blessed them He was parted from them and taken up into heaven.

We can imagine just what kind of a time it was to Him to arrive at His home one more time and behold His throne that had been vacant for more than thirty years. I wonder just what the angels did when he arrived at the gates of the Beautiful City. Of course He was not a stranger to them, but He had been away on the most interesting mission that a man ever went on, and He had been gone for thirty years. But He did not go back just as He came down, for He took five wounds with Him. He had the nail prints in His hands, and the prints of the spikes through His feet, and the spear print in His side, and I imagine that the angels stood and looked on in amazement and wondered what He had been through while He was out on the mission for us. Well, I suppose that while he told of the redemption of man the angels stood breathless. That was something new to them, for such a thing had never been heard of before until that day. But man who was lost and ruined by the fall and ruled by the devil, was bought back, and the way opened up whereby man might be brought back into perfect harmony with God. Man and his Creator could once more be reconciled, the one to the other. That was all provided for before the Christ ever walked off from the mountain top. He would have been here until now if He had not provided a remedy, but thank God, the remedy was provided, and man went out free and happy as a lark if he will accept the redemption provided by the blessed Son of God while he hung on the cross of Calvary.

When we think of all that took place in the life of Christ on the mountains of this earth, it is wonderful. We remember that He met the devil in His awful temptation on the mountain, and He preached the greatest sermon that the world ever heard or ever will hear on the top of the mountain, and He prayed all night on the mountain top and called His Apostles next morning, and He went to the top of Calvary with the cross on His shoulder to die for us, and He was transfigured on the mountain top, and He gave the commission to the disciples from the top of the mountain in Galilee. And now we see Him going back to the right hand of the Father from the mountain top.

These are among the greatest incidents in the life and death of Christ who came into a world on the most blessed mission that was ever heard of, and lived the most unselfish life that was ever heard of, and died the most cruel death that was ever heard of, and loved man so well that he was willing to let man put Him to death, and then died for the fellow who killed Him. The world tried to disgrace Him, and His life was so pure and spotless that disgrace would not stick to Him. His life was like the sunshine. The sun can shine all day on the mud hole in the road and at night withdraw itself without a blotch on it. The people said everything in the world about Him that was bad, and they accused Him of everything in the world that was bad, and He never disputed anything that was ever told on Him, and today three worlds believe Him to be innocent and the three worlds believe the world to be guilty. His life was as high above the life of men as the mountain tops are above the valleys. No compari-

Mount Olivet.   81

son at all; one on the top and the other on the bottom. As we see Him ascending the clouds we wonder what has become of the disgrace that was heaped on Him, The people said, "We heard Him say that He could destroy this temple and build it in three days," and they said that they heard Him say that He was the Son of God, and they said that they heard Him blaspheme, and they rent their clothes and cried out, "Away with him;" but after they had done all that a set of sin-cursed people could do—put Him to death, and put Him in the tomb, and put the stone over the mouth of the grave, and put the Roman soldiers there to guard it—on the third day after the crucifixion, we see Him get up and walk out of the tomb and we see the Roman soldiers tumbling over each other and falling like dead men.

In a few days we look up and behold, He is walking on the clouds and going back to the Father, and the High Priest and the Roman soldiers are just as helpless as the rest of us. But thank God, the little crowd that followed Him to Mount Olivet are as happy as the larks in the meadow and they have a shine on their faces and they have a promise that the rest of the folks haven't got. They come back to the city and go to the upper room and begin one of the most interesting prayer meetings that the world ever heard of, and they know that something will happen, for He said to them as He went up, "Behold I send the promise of the Father upon you; but tarry ye in the city of Jerusalem until ye be endued with power from on high. You were born of the flesh and were born of the Spirit, and have been baptized with water, and must be baptized with the Holy Ghost not many days hence." They knew that something was awaiting them, and so when the blessing did not get in on the first day they waited till the second, and till the third, and so on till the Day of Pentecost. They knew that there was something coming to them from on high, and bless the Lord, they waited for it and got it, and it was the blessed Holy Ghost.

CHAPTER XIV.

MOUNTAIN PEAKS OF LIFE—CONVICTION.

We have now come to the mountain peaks of life. There are at least three great mountain peaks in the life of every wholly sanctified man or woman. The first that stands out in the memory of the child of God is that experience of Bible Conviction. In the Christian experience Mount Sinai stands for conviction. You remember at Mount Sinai the Law was given and if so much as a beast touched the holy mountain it was thrust through with a dart. It is the same today; when the Holy Spirit convicts a sinner he is thrust through with a dart, and then he is ready to die to the world. He wants a place to pray, and he feels that he is the meanest man on earth, and he wonders why God has put up with him so long. He is amazed to think that God has kept him out of hell so long, and he is now ready to repent of his sins, and forsake his sins and believe on the Lord Jesus Christ.

When he does that he will hear from heaven; and until he hears the voice of God speaking to him as a loving Father, he hears the thunders of Mount Sinai and sees the forked lightning playing over his head, and knows that he is the man God is after. He knows that he is a hell-deserving wretch and that nothing but the grace of a merciful God has kept him out of the pit.

Now the little piece of dirt that he pays taxes on is as nothing in his own sight, and his bank stock is as nothing before him. It is not more horses and more mules that he wants, but it is God that he wants, for the man is under Bible conviction, and nothing short of a Bible repentance and a Bible confession and a Bible forsaking will bring peace to his troubled soul, but if he will meet God's conditions he will receive God's pardon. He has been thinking all the time that he was as good as anybody else, but today if you were to ask him about himself, he would tell you of a different man to what he thought he was a few days ago. He now has his eyes open.

The first thing that Bible conviction does for a fellow is to open his eyes, and for the first time in his life he sees himself as he really is. He has been thinking that he was one of the nicest men in the community, and as to his goodness, he never had a doubt about it until now. He thought he was as good as any church member in the community, and, in fact, he has often

Mount Peaks of Life.—Conviction. 85

said that he would not swap chances with the best of them for he said that he was an honest man, and he said that he paid all his debts, and he said that he had wronged no man, and he said that he had provided for his family a little better than the church members, and, in fact, he was all that could be desired of a gentleman. But the Master said, "Ye must be born again," and he has paid no attention to that, and all the time he has been boasting his own honesty. To his surprise when the arrow from the King's bow strikes him in the heart, and his eyes fly open, he sees down in his own heart that he is as tough as a meat block.

There in the natural heart, he sees anger, and jealousy, and pride and enmity and impatience, and profanity, and vulgarity, and Sabbath desecration, and the love of the world, and the love of praise, and the love of money, and no time for God, and no time for the Bible, and no time for prayer, and no time for God's house and no time for the service of the blessed Son of God. When all of this begins to dawn on the fellow, he thinks that he is the meanest white man on the face of the whole earth, and wonders how God can have mercy on him and save him at all. Some men I have seen almost go into despair when they see down in their own hearts, and all along before that they thought that they didn't need anything at all, and wondered why their friends were so interested in them.

One reason that we have so little spiritual life in the Church is because there is so little conviction, or maybe none at all. They have joined the church when the crowd went in, but nobody gets Bible religion just because the crowd is going that way. We must be convicted of our sins and wake up to the fact that we are lost, and when we wake up and find we are lost, then we are ready to start back to the Father's house. One thing that I do thank God for, and it is that I got a good case of Bible conviction and that I did repent of my sins, and confess my sins and forsake my sins, and then it was no trouble to believe on the Lord Jesus Christ, and thank God it was no trouble for Him to blot out all of my sins, and then give me the witness of the Spirit that I was the child of God. Well, amen, and amen.

CHAPTER XV.

MOUNT OF CONVERSION.

We have now come to the second mountain peak in the life of a sanctified Christian. Of course it is Conversion or the Witness of the Spirit, or Regeneration, or the New Birth, or being Born Again. All the above names are applied to the converted man.

As we saw that Mount Sinai was the mountain peak of conviction for the sinner, we see that Mount Calvary is the mountain peak for the regenerated man. It is a fact that when a man goes to Mount Sinai and gets under Bible conviction he goes down through the valley of repentance and climbs the mountain on which the cross stood, and there, all sin-cursed and devil-ridden he looks up through his tears and sees the blessed Son of God bleeding on Calvary for him. He there believes on him and then accepts Him as His Savior, and the load of conviction that has been hanging over his head ever since he left Mount Sinai, with all of his guilt, slips away at the foot of the cross on Calvary. Then and there he is pardoned and receives the witness of the Spirit and knows for himself that he is converted.

He knows that the load of guilt and condemnation rolled away on the mountain, and now he is a free man so far as sins are concerned, and he knows that he is a live man as far as life is concerned, for he has been born again. He has been changed from nature to grace. Old things have passed away, and behold all things are become new. He is now a new creature. He is what we called a justified man, or, to make it real plain he is now a religious man. He has been regenerated and has been adopted into the family of God. and his name has been written in the Lamb's Book of Life. Now if he keeps what he got, he will be alive a million years from today and shining in the Kingdom of our Lord Jesus Christ.

The regenerated life is one of the great mountain peaks of the life of a man of God. It is a great thing to be born again. Indeed it is so great that so many have supposed that there is no room for anything else, and they have made the mistake of trying to make the new birth cover all the ground of the life of the Christian. I am ready and willing to admit that regeneration goes as far as God intended regeneration to go, but God never intended regeneration to cover the ground that sanctification is to cover. If we look we will see that there is a vast difference between the birth of the Spirit and the baptism of the Spirit.

We are all convinced that it is one of the great things of the great God to regenerate a dead soul, but thank God, He can do it, and not only that, be He can give you the witness of the Spirit to the work that has been done, and the man who has received it will know it a little better than he knows anything else.

But while we call regeneration one mountain peak, there are nine works of grace in that one work, or somebody else would say, that there are nine steps to be taken to get out of sin into the life of righteousness. I can give them to you just so plain that anybody on earth can see them.

To begin with here is the first step to be taken: it is Bible conviction. Don't you see that conviction is one thing, and regeneration is another? Now after a man is convicted he repents of his sins. So you see that repentance is one thing and regeneration is another. Well now, when the fellow repents of his sins he is brought to the place where he confesses his sins, and you see that to confess is one thing and regeneration is another. But take another step. After he confesses his sins he is brought to the place where he can believe on the Lord Jesus Christ. You see at a glance that regeneration is one thing and to believe on the Lord Jesus Christ is another. Well now, when a man believes on the Lord Jesus Christ he is then and there justified. We understand that justification must take place in the mind of God, and before he can count that man just He must look at him through the blood of His own Son. When he is justified in the mind of God, He sends the Holy Spirit to witness to it, and we call that regeneration. He is born again, or regenerated, and when he is regenerated, the Holy Spirit will come into his heart bearing witness with his heart that he is now the child of God. Now there is justification, or being justified from past guilt, and there is regeneration, or the making alive of a dead soul, and there is the witness of the Spirit that these works of grace are done in your heart. When that is done then and there you are adopted into the family of God, and your name is written in the Lamb's Book of Life.

Now reader, if you will look you will see nine works of grace as plain as the sunshine before your eyes. Now let us state the nine works as they come in order to make it real plain. First conviction, and second repentance, third confession, fourth forsaking, fifth believing, sixth justification, seventh regeneration,

Mount of Conversion. 91

eighth the witness of the Spirit, ninth **adoption.** It takes all of these great works in the life of the man to make a Bible Christian out of him and get him started on the road to heaven I grant you that the above looks like enough to make a man anything in the world that he ought to be, but you will notice that there is not one thing said in all of the above works of grace concerning the carnal mind, or the Old Man as he is called, and the blessing, as great as it is, only deals with the sins that we have committed. There is not one thing in the above to show that the Old Man is destroyed in regeneration, but there are thousands of things in the life of the churchmembers of the present time to show that, as the Bible puts it, they are "yet carnal," and it has ever been so.

A regenerated man today is as religious as they ever were in any other age of the world. The people who were born again 1900 years ago did not get any better religion than I got on the frontier of Texas 29 years ago. They needed The Blessing, and so did I, and so do you, and so do we all. But that is to be the next mountain peak that we are to discuss.

The real facts are that the regenerated life is a great life, and higher than the great bulk of people live. If we, as a people, were to live up to God's standard of regeneration, we would have no trouble in getting the Church into the experience of holiness. At the first opportunity they would go into the fountain as a drove of sheep over the pasture fence. You could not keep them out of the blessed experience of full salvation. If it were popular to be sanctified, in all the churches we would have them at the altar by the tens of thousands, and such a sevival would break out as the world never saw. The glory would fill the tabernacle and the world would be brought to Christ in this generation.

CHAPTER XVI.

MOUNT OF SANCTIFICATION.

We have now come to the third mountain peak in the life of the Christian, and of course it is the blessing of sanctification. We have noticed that Mount Sinai stands for conviction and that Mount Calvary stands for regeneration. So Mount Zion stands for sanctification. We read in the 24th chapter of St. Luke's Gospel and the 49th verse: "And behold I send the promise of my Father upon you. But tarry ye in the city of Jerusalem until ye be endued with power from on high." Here we have the promise of the Father. Christ Himself says that the Father had promised the blessing, and for them to tarry at Jerusalem until the blessing came. The Lord knew that these men could not do the work that was before them until they had received power from on high. He Himself called it the enduement of power and He never said it was to be in the schools, for He knew too well that the schools had nothing to give. There is no use in the world for a beggar to hang around a fellow who hasn't anything to give. The Master was honest with us and said that the enduement of power was to come down to us from on high.

You remember that St. James said that "If any man lack wisdom, let him ask of the Lord, who giveth to all men liberally and upbraideth not, and it shall be given him." James understood that not only the power is to come down from on high, but that the wisdom was to come down from on high also. The Master said that, "Ye must be born again," so even the spiritual birth is not of this world, but is like wisdom and power, it must come down from the great Fountain Head, the Father of all life, and light, and wisdom, and power, and goodness, and love, and mercy.

John the Baptist in the 3rd of Matthew says that the believer is to be baptized with the Holy Ghost and fire is not the new birth, for a fellow must be born before he can be baptized. We read in the Gospel of St. John 14:16: "And I will pray the Father and he will give you another Comforter that he may abide with you forever." Here John says that when we receive Him that He is the Abiding Comforter. Well, he means to say that when we receive the Holy Ghost He will come to abide with us, and that He is a comforter. We all know that is the very thing that we want and must have if we ever succeed in the work of the Master.

To keep what we have is not to succeed, and to just hold our own is not a success at all. To succeed, we must not only keep what we have, and hold all we have gained, but we must go on and take new territory each day. If our camp fires are found in the same place for as long as two nights, we are not traveling, but are standing still. To stand means to go back, for if we don't go forward, we must go backward. Going to heaven is like riding the bicycle; you have to go on or get off one or the other. The faster it runs, the straighter it stands, and the slower it goes, the worse it wabbles, and when it stops it falls.

We read again in Matt. 14:26: "But the Comforter which is the Holy Ghost, whom the Father will send in my name, he shall teach you all things and bring all things to your remembrance whatsoever I have said unto you." The Holy Ghost is a Comforter and also a teacher. His office work is to comfort and impart knowledge; He is our Instructor or Teacher. And notice, the Master said that He will bring all things to your remembrance. He will not let us forget anything. He is a constant reminder that "the Master said so and so." We are to have all the promise and all the will fulfilled in us, and as long as there is anything coming to us from our Father's will, the blessed Holy Ghost will remind us of it, and will never stop until we get all that is coming to us.

Now reader, I think that it is simply grand. How badly we need such a teacher here in this world of sin and sorrow where the devil is doing all that a mighty devil can do to teach men the way of sin and death. One way that he has been successful is to keep men in ignorance of the good things that God has in store for them. Most of the people are living away down below their blessed privileges. The devil has been able to keep them from getting in possession of their great estate, and as long as he can succeed in that he is not only defeating them, but he is defeating the blessed Son of God who bought the blessing for us with His own blood. Of course we know that every child of God can have the blessing the very day that he comes for it, and brings himself to the Lord. The blessing will then and there be delivered to him. For the work of the blessed Holy Ghost is to teach the child of God and bring these things to his remembrance, and the main thing that is to be brought to his mind is the blessing of sanctification.

From the time the young convert starts to heaven the blessed Holy Ghost begins to draw him into his own companionship and begins to teach him of the Christ and what He is able to do for him. I have seen Christians by the thousands who wanted to be filled with all the fullness of God. The blessed Holy Ghost had done His office work in their hearts, and they were so hungry for the blessing that they could hardly stand it. I have known them to go to their pastors and tell them of the hunger in their hearts, and instead of the pastors leading the flock of God into the green pastures, they would lead them the other way and tell them that it is impossible for them to have an experience that would satisfy their poor hungry souls and turn them away empty. Well, you will find such a preacher described in the prophecy of Ezekiel where he said, "Woe be unto the shepherds" who feed themselves and beat or shear or starve the flock.

So many places I go I find that the most of the church members are away ahead of their pastors, and instead of the pastors leading the flock, as the Lord is my judge, they are in the way of their own people and are a drawback to them instead of a blessing. I go to plenty of places where the only hope of a revival in the church is the prayers of a few faithful ones, and the pastor is in the way from the time the meeting opens till it closes. If he would get up and leave town or stay away from the meeting it would be far better for the church. I know that my statement is not overdrawn although some people might think so, but it is because they do not see the conditions as we see them.

The blessed Holy Ghost will not work where He is to take a back seat, and His work is not to be made light of either by the preacher or the workers. Where the blessed Holy Ghost can have perfect right of way, He will convict sinners and regenerate believers and sanctify His own people and fill them with Himself and make their lives happy and useful and make them a blessing to the world in which they live.

Now we read in St. John 15:26, 27: "But when the comforter is come whom I will send unto you from the Father, even the Spirit of truth, which proceedeth from the Father, he shall testify of me and ye also shall bear witness because you have been with me from the beginning." The reader will notice that when we receive the blessed Holy Ghost He is to testify of Christ, and we also are to bear witness. There is no way for a man to find out about Christ, but by the Holy Ghost. The man may read the Bible for years and be as ignorant of Christ as a heathen; he may never know the blessed Son of God until the Holy Spirit comes to his heart and bears witness to the truth that he has been reading in the Bible. You have

Mount of Sanctification. 99

read of Christ in the Book, but until the Holy Ghost reveals the Christ to you, you will have nothing more or less than a piece of history in your mind. But bless God, when the blessed Holy Ghost comes to your heart, you will know the Son of God better than you will know the voice of your mother. That is the beauty of the incoming Holy Ghost, and from now you will have a testimony and the glory of the Lord will be there to bless you and to keep you and to guide you into all truth and to comfort you and to fight your battles and to defeat your enemies and to encourage you and to help you to bear the burdens of life.

I am so thankful to know that we have this wonderful Treasure, and that He is to abide with us forever. We are to never be without Him and His abiding presence again while we live. Well, glory to God! that is enough to put all the Church at the mourners' bench as a set of seekers for Him, the blessed Comforter and Teacher, and the one who is to testify to the truth of God and His Christ and His revealed Word. For Paul says in the 12th Chapter of 1st Corinthians that "no man can say that Jesus is the Lord but by the Holy Ghost," so beloved, we must have the Holy Ghost in order to know the Son of God, and we must have the Son of God before we know the Father.

So all the steps in the divine life are only possible through the Holy Ghost. We must be convicted by the Holy Ghost and we must be born of the Spirit, and we must be baptized by the Holy Ghost and fire, and we must have the Holy Ghost to know the Son, and we must have the Son to know the Father.

Now we want to look at some beautiful things in St. John's Gospel 16:7. 8. Christ said to the disciples: "Nevertheless, I tell you the truth it is expedient for you that I go away, for if I go not away the Comforter will not come unto you, but if I depart I will send him unto you. And when he is come he will reprove the world of sin and of righteousness and of judgment." The reader will notice in the above text that the only way that God ever convicts sinners is to send the Holy Ghost into the heart and life of the believers. You notice that Christ said it was expedient for us that He went away, for He said, "If I go not away the Comforter will not come to you but if I depart I will send him." Well now, the question naturally arises in the mind of the reader, when the Holy Ghost is come where will he come? Or in other words, where will He stay if he comes? We will say as the Bible directs, there is but one place for the Holy Ghost to come, and that is to the heart of the regenerated child of God for we know that the Holy Ghost can't come and live in the hearts of sinners.

Christ says when the Holy Ghost comes and takes up His abode in the hearts of the children of God that sinners will be convicted of sin and of righteousness and of the Judgment, so at a glance we see the only hope in the universe for a sinner is for God's people to go down before Him and get filled with the Holy Ghost, and when they do it the sinners will come flocking home to God by the tens of thousands. You may take the sinners of the community and they think that they are all right and don't need a thing, but when the children of God go to the altar and make their consecration and receive the Holy Ghost the sinner will then and there get his eyes open, and at once he will see that he is a guilty sinner and on the road to an awful hell. He has been thinking that he was as righteous as anybody, but when he gets under conviction he will find out that he hasn't any righteousness at all. Then in that condition he will wake up to the fact that he is judgment day bound, and he will see that he is not prepared for it at all. Then there is some hope of him. Until now he has been blind as a bat, but now he sees his condition.

Now we read the 13th verse of this 16th chapter and we have a beautiful statement. "Howbeit when the spirit of truth is come he will guide you into all truth for he shall not speak of himself, but whatsoever he shall hear, that shall he speak, and he will shew you things to come." Here the reader will notice that the Holy Ghost is to be a guide. In the other scriptures that we have read He was to be a comforter, and a teacher, and a testifier, and a revealer of Christ. How beautiful all the above scriptures are. Now we come to the one that shows Him to be more than all the above. He is here shown as a guide and how important it is that we have a guide, for we are to be pilgrims and strangers here below, for here we have no continuing city, but we seek one to come, whose builder and maker is God.

As we pass through this wilderness we need a guide, and thank the Lord, we are to have one, the blessed Holy Ghost. How beautiful it is to know that we are to have a comforter, and a teacher, and a revealer, and a testifier, and a guide, all in the person of the Holy Ghost. Not only that, but we notice in the same verse that He is to show us things to come. Here the blessed Holy Ghost is to become to us a prophet and tell us things that are to come. To us that looks reasonable, for we read that

Mount of Sanctification.   103

the holy men of old spake as they were moved by the Holy Ghost, and if the Holy Ghost could tell a man things that were to come to pass a thousand years before it did come to pass, we see that He could make known things to us as well. So the blessed Holy Ghost is to be everything to us that we need to get us out of a life of sin into a life of righteousness and holiness, and finally into heaven, for He is to comfort us on the way, and He is to teach us on the way, and He is to take the things of Christ and show them to us on the way.

Well, if He will do all that, it looks like we might get through, don't it? It does to me, bless His holy name. The way all seems so clear to a fellow when he has heard from the skies and knows for himself and not for another that the Holy Ghost will take the things of Christ and show them to us. There will be no trouble if we will look, and if we won't look the loss will be ours and not His, and every mouth will be stopped before God.

Now reader, we come to the 14th verse of the 16th Chapter of St. John's Gospel. "He shall glorify me, for he shall receive of mine and shall shew it unto you." Now the blessed Son of God tells us that when the Holy Ghost is come that He will glorify Him, and the great bulk of the church members of this country are trying some new scheme to see if they can't glorify the blessed Christ. But everything that is tried proves to be a flat failure and is no good in the world. It comes to naught because they have gone to the wrong thing to bring glory to the blessed Christ. If they will go down on their knees now and receive the Holy Ghost they will be in the line or on the way to success, for just as sure as they get the Holy Ghost and live the life they will bring glory to the blessed Son of God. The way to glorify the Christ is to get the Holy Ghost.

Now notice what the Christ said, "He, (the Holy Ghost) shall take the things of mine and shall shew them unto you." One way for us to bring glory and honor to the life of Christ is to let the Holy Ghost take the things of Christ and show them unto us. What an honor the blessed Son of God confers on us. Just think of it, the Holy Ghost taking the things of Christ and showing them to us. Just think of it, if a poor man of America were to go to England and King Edward were to have the man brought in and show him all the glory and honor that belonged to that great nation, the man would never get over talking about it in the world. But here the King of kings and Lord of lords offers to have the Holy Ghost take the things of His and show them to us.

Mount of Sanctification. 105

The Bible speaks of the "riches of his glory." Don't you know that it is wonderful to behold the glory of a great king here in this world? And just think of the glory of the blessed Son of God, all of which you are to behold and enjoy just as if you were your very own. I don't wonder that the Apostle cried out, "Oh the depth of the riches of the glory of the Son of God." It is said to be past finding out. Of course it is, and we never would find it out if the blessed Holy Ghost did not take them and show them to us. We don't discover them; they are shown to us by the Spirit.

We come now to the scriptures that show the Holy Ghost as our baptizer. You may read St. Matthews 3:11 first and see how the scriptures harmonize. Notice the reading of this, "I indeed baptize you with water unto repentance, but he that cometh after me is mightier than I whose shoes I am not worthy to bear, he shall baptize you with the Holy Ghost and with fire." Now we turn to St. Mark's Gospel 1:8: "I indeed have baptized you with water, but he shall baptize you with the Holy Ghost." Now we turn to Luke's Gospel 3:16: "John answered, saying to them all, I indeed baptize you with water, but one mightier than I cometh, the latchet of whose shoes I am not worthy to unloose. He shall baptize you with the Holy Ghost and with fire." Now turn and read the next lesson from John's Gospel, 1:33: "And I knew him not, but he that sent me to baptize with water the same said unto me, Upon whom thou shalt see the Spirit descending and remaining on him, the same is he which baptizes with the Holy Ghost." And then John adds in the next verse, "And I saw and bear record that this is the Son of God."

So that settles forever who it is that is to baptize with the Holy Ghost; it is the blessed Son of God. But we turn now and read Acts 1:5: "For John truly baptized with water, but ye shall be baptized with the Holy Ghost not many days hence." In connection with the scriptures we have already used, we will read the 8th verse of the first chapter of Acts: "But ye shall receive power after that the Holy Ghost is come upon you, and ye shall be witnesses unto me both in Jerusalem and in all Judea and in Samaria and unto the uttermost parts of the earth." Now reader, a Christian experience that will reach to the uttermost parts of the earth is to my mind a mountain-peak experience, or a mountain-top life. There is no use for me to undertake to explain the above scriptures, for they don't need anybody to explain them. They only need a fellow to believe them and go to shouting the victory through the blessed Son of God, and we are ready to do that now, and if we have got the blessed experience, it won't be long until it will break out on us and somebody will know it, and then somebody else will hear about it, and the first thing you know it will be all over the settlement, and then all over the state, and then to the uttermost parts of the earth.

CHAPTER XVII.

THE DOOMED CITY.

Dear reader, we now come to the Doomed City and the family of Lot making their escape from the city of Sodom. The text is Gen. 19:17. "And it came to pass when they had brought them forth abroad that he said, Escape for thy life, look not behind thee neither stay thou in all the plain; escape to the mountains lest thou be consumed." The reader will notice that when the angel led Lot and his family out of Sodom that he said, "Escape for thy life," and he said it because the city was doomed to destruction. In this case the city of Sodom stands for a life of sin. All sin is doomed and all sin will be destroyed, and it makes no difference whom God finds sin on, he is a doomed man and will be destroyed if he don't make his escape from the doomed city. All sin is to the Lord today just what Sodom was that day.

I suppose one sin deliberately committed against God is as distasteful and as disgusting and as destructive in its make-up as ten thousand of the same kind would be committed against God. You may take any line of sin that you can think of, and the thing is as much doomed as Sodom was, and as surely as old Sodom went down under the flames of the wrath of a sin-avenging God, that line of sin is doomed to go the same way. You may think of what the world would call a nice line of sin, such as dancing and card playing and theatre going, and circus running, and Sabbath desecration, and lodgeism, and tobaccoism, and the race course, and liquor in all of its hideous forms, and the world thinks that these things are a part of the necessities of life, and can see no sin in them at all. But nevertheless they are a brood of doomed sinners just waiting for the angel to come out with the sword of God in his hand and pronounce the awful curse of the Almighty on the whole herd. So it is run or burn, one or the other, for all Sodom is doomed and the angels are now on their way to this earth to destroy old Sodom again, and all the Lot family will have to escape or go down in the flames and be used as fuel to feed the flames with.

So the angel got the man Lot by the hand and said, "Escape for thy life and look not behind thee, neither stay thou in all the plain lest thou be consumed." Remember Lot said, "Oh no, my Lord." But the angel took noth-

The Doomed City. 111

ing back. It was escape or perish, for the angels were there, and they were there for the one purpose, and that was to destroy Sodom.

If the reader will turn to the 13th Chapter of Matthew and read verses 41 and 42 he will have the destruction of Sodom told over again. Notice the reading of these two verses. "The Son of man shall send forth his angels and they shall gather out of his kingdom all things that offend and them that do iniquity, and shall cast them in a furnace of fire; there shall be wailing and gnashing of teeth." The reader will notice that the angels were used of the Lord to destroy Sodom, and now Christ tells that at the last day the angels will be used to gather out of His Kingdom all things that offend and them who do iniquity and cast them into a furnace of fire.

Again the reader will remember that when God wanted to destroy all the first-born of Egypt that He sent out the destroying angel and a mighty wail went up from Egypt for there was one dead in every home. You will find it recorded in Exodus 12:29, 30.

Again you will remember when the King of Assyria went up to make war against Israel that he went in the name of the gods that he had made with his own hands, and he defied the God of the Israelites and told them to not let Hezekiah deceive them, for he said that there was no God who could deliver Israel out of his hand. He wrote a letter to the King of Israel in which he defied the God of heaven, and when Hezekiah got the letter he went to the top of the wall of Jerusalem and spread the letter out before the Lord and told Him to read the letter that King Sennacherib had written. And the Lord read the letter and that night He sent out one of His mighty angels, and the next morning there were dead men almost without number. Just turn and read Isaiah 37:36: "Then the angel of the Lord went forth and smote in the camp of the Assyrians 185,000, and when they arose early in the morning behold they were all dead corpses." Now reader, that looks like business to see one angel out in a single night leaving 185,000 dead men on the plains.

Just think of old Sodom now, and look and see, the angels are already in the city, and leading out Lot and his family. The city is doomed, but God loved one man and his name was Abraham, and he had prayed for Lot, and for Abraham's sake God spared Lot, but he destroyed the city.

The next clause in this text that we will look at is this "Look not behind thee." It is not well pleasing to the Lord for a man to start to

The Doomed City.

the land of righteousness or to the hills of safety and then turn and look at the thing he had to give up. Sodom was doomed and God had said, "Escape for thy life," and now if the city is doomed and the curse of God is hanging over it and He is now ready to rain fire from heaven on the city and burn it up, as He will all sin, it is not pleasing to Him to see a fellow start and then turn and look back at the city or his old life of sin.

How many times have we seen the young man or the young lady start for heaven and for some time make a splendid run, and then turn back to the old life and become harder and get further away from God than they were before they started. They have looked back at Sodom. You remember Lot's wife. She turned and looked back and never took another step in the right direction. She was left standing there as a warning to all who should come after her that it was dangerous to leave and then turn and look back at the thing that we have to give up. It is like this. When Lot and his family left Sodom they had started to another city, and now when they lose enough interest in the city that they are going to, to stop and look back at the one they have left, right then and there they are backslidden, for their interest should not be in the city behind them but in the city before them. God had commanded them to flee from Sodom and He said look not behind thee. Don't even stop to look back at old Sodom, for she is doomed and will be destroyed. And if you hang around Sodom and I destroy Sodom I will destroy you with the city. We are to escape or we are to perish, one or the other.

No doubt that the devil met Lot's wife as he did Mother Eve and said to her, "Did the Lord command that you should not look back at the city?" "Yes," said she to him, "that was the command." "Well," said the devil, "just look yonder. Don't you see the house of your children on fire? Just listen to their cries. It is a shame for the Lord to treat them that way." And Mrs. Lot turned herself and took the last look at the city, and she never looked again, and never will in this world, for the Old Book says that there she was turned to a pillar of salt.

The next step that we take in the text is this: "Stay not thou in the plain." The idea that we get from this clause in the text is this: The Lord don't want us to stay too close to the place where we started from. He said, "And stay not thou in all the plain." There is danger of a fellow staying too close to his old crowd. If he don't watch they will get him back into his

The Doomed City. 115

old life. Old Sodom, or the old life, or the old crowd are all kin to the Old Man, or the carnal mind, and if we undertake to stay too close they will have us back in the old city before we know it. Our only hope is to get up and flee from the doomed city, and then not even stop and look back at the hateful thing, and then not stay too close to the city when we get out.

I have seen young ladies who had been well nigh ruined by the ball room, weep their way to the altar, and weep over their lives of waywardness and confess out to God and forsake the thing, and sweet peace would come into their lives and they would run well for awhile. But it would not be six months till the devil and his crowd would have them go to a nice play party, all the time telling them there was no harm in a nice play party. Then the old life would begin to grip them like a mighty monster from the forest, and in a few weeks you will hear of them at one of the nice balls up town. Well, she is now back in Sodom, and will probably stay right there till Sodom is destroyed, and she will go down in the flames never to rise again. Don't you see she did not heed God' command? He said, "Escape for thy life." He said, "Look not behind thee." And He also said, "And stay thou in all the plains lest thou be consumed." Well, she looked back, and she wanted to go back, and she did not go on, and of course she turned back and is still back, and will probably stay back. Well, you say, "Back where?" Back in old Sodom, or the old life of sin, just where she was before she ever made a start, and she is harder to reach today than she was before she ever left Sodom the first time. The devil has a harder grip on her than he ever had in this world. How much it means to escape from the old life, and then not stop on the plains, or look back, or anything of the kind, but it is possible, or God would never have given such a command, and the reason He did it was for our good and our protection and safety.

The next clause in the text is this, now notice it: "Escape to the mountain lest thou be consumed." The reader will notice that we now have already had one escape, and now we have another. That makes up the two escapes in this verse. First He said, "Escape from the doomed city." That is, without a doubt, the sinner escaping from the life of sin, and then He said, "Look not behind thee," and then he said, "Neither stay thou in all the plains," and now He says, "Escape to the mountains lest thou be consumed."

Fleeing from Sodom is nothing more or less

than the sinner giving up his old life of sin and fleeing to the Savior for salvation. The plains that God told him not to stay on are, without a doubt, the plains of regeneration, or the justified life. The lesson, with many others, teaches that it is not God's will for the believer to undertake to live the justified life alone very long, for God told him to not only get out of Sodom, but He told him not to stay on the plains, and then He added, "Escape to the mountains lest thou be consumed." The tide of worldliness is so strong today that if a man tries to live in the average church and do as they do it will not be twelve months until they will have you back in the old life or back into Sodom. The Lord knew that He made provision for us to have an experience that would enable us to stand in the face of all kinds of opposition, and notice this statement, the Lord said if we did not escape from the plains, that we would be consumed. He was not talking to somebody in Sodom, he was talking to us who have fled from the old life of sin, or Sodom. So we see at a glance that it was not the Lord's will for us to try to live the life of a complete Christian until we were wholly sanctified.

The old life in Sodom represents the life of a sinner, escaping from the doomed city and getting out on the plains, is a type of a justified life, and the escaping to the mountain top is a type of the sanctified life. It is called the higher life, it is called the fullness of the blessing, it is called holiness, it is called sanctification, and it is called perfect love, it is called a clean heart, it is called the baptism with the Holy Ghost, it is called the crucifixion of the Old Man. Some call it the power for service. But whatever it may be called, He said, "Escape to the mountain."

There is nothing more lovely than the mountain-top life. Think of it in this light: if there is any sunshine anywhere it is found on the mountain top; and again, if there is any pure air in the whole country it is found on the mountain top; if a man gets sick his doctor will advise him at once to go to the mountain and get the fine mountain air. He tells him to go up to the mountain top and get some ozone, and the poor fellow will ask the doctor to tell him what ozone is, and the doctor says that it is a double portion of oxygen. Then he is teaching the second blessing to his patients. Well, another way to look at it: if there are such things as mosquitoes anywhere in the country, they will be found down on the plains; and if there are any croaking frogs anywhere in the whole country, they will be found down on the plains; but if you will get up and flee to the mountain

The Doomed City.

top you will get out of hearing of the humming mosquitoes and alligators. All of these things go in to make up the life of the unsanctified Christian. The average Christian is almost annoyed to death with the little things of life, when it is God's will and purpose for him to live above such things. A drove of mosquitoes will come in the form of anger and pride and jealousy and impatience, and the little things that annoy and hinder the Christian who lives down on the plain until he has no rest day or night. But the Lord said, "Escape to the mountain lest thou be consumed." Brother, the frogs and bugs of different kinds will consume you if you don't escape.

Again, from the mountain top we get such a fine view of all the surrounding country. Just think of it in this light: a man down on the plains can't see anywhere, but a man on the mountain top can see for hundreds of miles away, and the views from the mountain top are just lovely. You see far out on the plains that lie in the valley below you if you are on the top of the great old mountain. I don't wonder that the Lord wanted us to push onto the mountain top and bathe in the pure and warm sunshine and get a good view of all the world around about us.

> I can see far down the mountain,
> Where I wandered many years;
> Often hindered in my journey
> By the ghosts of doubts and fears,
> Broken vows and disappointments,
> Thickly sprinkled all the way,
> But the Spirit led unerring,
> To the land I hold today.

Now again look at it in this light: if there are any clouds and fogs and mist and darkness, they always hang over the plain. At times the people down in the plains will have the most awful storms and the most awful thunder and lightning you ever heard, and the people on the mountain top will have the finest sunshine and the most lovely weather you ever saw. While the Christians who live down on the plains of regeneration fight mosquitoes and listen to the croaking of the frogs and see the fog and mist, the mountain-top Christian is delivered from the whole thing.

It is very seldom that the mountain-top Christian ever has a cloudy day, and so he sings:

> I am dwelling on the mountain,
> Where the golden sunlight gleams.

There is no comparison on earth between the Christian down in the plains struggling with his doubts and fears, and the Christian on the mountain top with his skies all bright and clear

The Doomed City. 121

and the glory of God in his soul and his life hid with Christ in God and Jesus in all of His fullness and sweetness dwelling in his soul. The mountain-top Christian has bright sunshine, and he has pure air to breathe, and he has a good vision of the surrounding country, and he is away from the mosquitoes, and away from the frogs, and he is above the fog and mist, and he very seldom sees a cloud. If you will compare these things to the life of the average Christian you will find that the most of them have never left the plains and they have stayed down there so long until they don't think they can get away. If we ask them to come up the mountain with us, they will tell you that they can't get up the mountain, and if we offer to help them up they will make all kinds of excuses, and while they fight mosquitoes and bull-gnats and dog-flies and bumblebees and hornets, and grope in the darkness and mist and fog, they will tell you that they got it all at once.

Yet the Lord said, "Escape to the mountain lest thou be consumed." The little things of this life are just about to provoke them to death. Well, just watch them; they are going to the mountain top, or they are going back to old Sodom, one or the other.

CHAPTER XVIII.

GOD'S HOLY MOUNTAIN.

As we have been on the beautiful mountain of the Bible, here is one of the beautiful sayings of the gospel prophet, Isaiah. He seemed to see things that nobody else saw in his day, and he said things that nobody else said. Just listen to him here in chapter 11:9: "They shall not hurt nor destroy in all my holy mountain, for the earth shall be full of the knowledge of the Lord as the waters cover the sea." There is no way to make a man's language more beautiful than the above. This one verse proves this man to be inspired, a Spirit-filled man, and a God-called man, and a God-sent man.

The text is the life of sanctification in the hearts of the people at some period of the world. While it is broad enough to take in the whole world it is so narrow that one man can get the blessing and live the life and enjoy the experience and teach the doctrine if nobody else in the country wants it. But he speaks of this holy mountain, and in this holy mountain he says that nothing shall hurt or destroy, and then he adds that the earth shall be full of the knowledge of the Lord as the waters cover the sea. This reaches out and beyond the community and marks a day that this old world will be brought into perfect harmony with the principles of the Gospel of the blessed Son of God.

While this is so, the earth will be covered with men and women who have been born of the Spirit and then baptized with the Spirit, and filled with the fullness of God. There will be no sinners on the earth at that time, and that is what we all want to see. The only reason that heaven is heaven is because there's no sin there. If sin were in heaven, it would be no better than Chicago or New York, but thank the Lord, there is one city that the devil can't control, and never will, for it is the home of God, and therefore it is the home of the children of God. That being the case, there is no sin or devil in that beautiful city. If the reason that heaven is so beautiful is because there is no sin there, wouldn't this country be just as lovely as heaven if the devil and sin were put out of it? Well, that is the very thing the old prophet saw in his wonderful vision, a world redeemed by the blood of the Son of God, and delivered from the clutches of a mighty devil.

There is in the minds of the holy people all over the country a time in the future referred

God's Holy Mountain. 125

to as the thousand years, or millennium, or the reign of Christ on the earth, and if this is right, this is the time that the old prophet had in mind when he saw a world free from danger and delivered from the devil and full of the knowledge of the Lord as the waters cover the sea. There must be a glorious time in the near future for the children of God, for their lives have been sorely tried.

How many mothers have raised sons for no purpose only the saloon and the gambling house, and have raised beautiful daughters for no purpose only for the bawdy house, and when and how can that precious mother ever get revenge out of sin and the devil for her great and awful loss? I know that some people say she will be delivered from the devil when she gets to heaven, but the text says that, "They shall not hurt nor destroy in all his holy mountain," and that the earth is to be "full of the knowledge of the Lord as the waters cover the sea," and this earth is not heaven, and heaven is not this earth, and if this earth is to be the heaven there is but one way to do it and that is to put the devil off of this planet, and remove all sin, and remove all sinners, and then we would have just what the old prophet saw, a world free from the devil and all of his subjects.

We all know and rejoice in the fact that

God has provided a plan of redemption, that man may be saved from all sin and kept by the power of God, but while he is kept he will be tempted a thousand times in a single week to do the very thing he knows that if he does do it will ruin him in two worlds. He has the tempter to fight and reject day and night, and if he slows up he goes back to the bottom again, must do all of his first works over again or be forever lost. But the prophet saw a day coming when all will be different. I know that there is a better day for this old world for it is described in the blessed old Book, and I am hungry today to see things changed, and I am anxious to get into a world where the devil won't be boss and general manager, and thank God, I am expecting to get into just such a world some day as is described in the above text, a world of glory, a world of love, a world of kindness and filled with the redeemed of the Lord. In that day there will be no danger, for the lion will be as tame as the calf, and the tiger will be as gentle as the lamb, the serpent will be as harmless as the beautiful butterfly. I know that such things are very hard to believe by the most of the human family, but a man who has ever been touched by the Holy Ghost, is ready to believe all that God says, and here is a statement that is so beautiful that

Gods Holy Mountain.   127

you want to sell out and move over there at once and if we can't sell we are just about ready to give away all that we have.

Just listen once more to the voice of the prophet: "They shall not hurt nor destroy in all my holy mountain, for the earth shall be full of the knowledge of the Lord as the waters cover the sea." Now reader, that day has never been fulfilled yet. It has to this extent, some few people have received the blessed experience of scriptural holiness, and as far as they are concerned the world is full of love at least. But it is very seldom that we can find a family in which every member is fully saved, and the few who are fully saved are so tempted and tried by the devil until they have little time to enjoy their experience; it takes all of their time to fight sin and the devil. There is no telling just what the experience would be to them if they had time from the awful onslaught of the devil to enjoy their experience. But in the present world if we sit down to enjoy our experience for a few days, we will wake up to the fact that we are backslidden.

We must fight here or die hereafter. The devil is after us, and if we stop the fight, he is the winner and we the loser. We sing here

>   Must I be carried to the skies
>   On flowery beds of ease,

> While others fought to win the prize
> And sailed through bloody seas.

The poet recognized the fact that we must turn or burn, fight or die, one or the other. But how different it will be in the world without a devil in it, and how different it will be in a world without sin in it, or a sinner in it. When you think of the sorrow of heaven and the horror of hell and the ruination of earth, as Bro. Will Huff used to say, just think of the devil and you have the key to the whole situation. But bless God, the old prophet saw a day coming when there will be a world with no devil in it, and we are looking forward to that great day. Amen.

CHAPTER XIX.

THE MOUNTAIN TOP OF SIN.

We have been talking of the mountain-top life of the saint, and it is surely beautiful. Nothing on earth to be compared to the life of full salvation. The life of the sinner is like the dark, rainy, drizzling night, and the life of the justified is like the beautiful moonshine on a lovely moonlight night, but the sanctified life is like the noon hour of a bright sunshiny day.

But for a little while we want to look at the mountain-top life of sin. If there is a life of faith and love that God could compare to a mountain top of glory, there must be a life of sin that would compare to a mountain. While one has a mountain of glory, and of love, and of peace, and of joy, and of rest, the other has a mountain of sorrow, and sadness, and misery, and woe, and dissatisfaction, and unrest, and his condemnation is piled up around him like a mountain.

He can look back over his past life and see many sins that he has committed that look like hills, and others that look like great mountains to him. At another time his sins look like an ocean of black ink, and as he sees them he gives up all hope and sinks down into dark despair. At another time he looks at his sins and they look like a herd of savage beasts, every one of them with fiery eyes just ready to tear him to pieces. As he listens to their awful growls the blood will almost freeze in his veins, and the devil will tell him that there is no hope for him in the world. At another time his sins are like a flock of vultures, and they flop their black, skinny wings in his poor face by day and by night, and when he works all day they will sit over his bed at night, and as he tries to sleep the devil will give him a few horrible nightmares. As he wakes out of his awful stupor the devil will tell him that the thing he needs is some more drink and that if he will get on one more big drunk his troubles will all disappear. Under the delusion of the devil he goes out to get on another drunk in order to drown his troubles. Then as he sobers up his sins will crawl around him and over him and entwine themselves about him like a herd of awful serpents, and while the doctor tells him that it is not real snakes but only the tremens, the poor man can feel a thousand awful snakes crawling up his back, and ove his bare body, and while he groans in awful agony, the Methodist stewards and Baptist

The Mountain Top of Sin.

deacons and the Presbyterian elders have voted to one of their neighbors what they call high license, and the bartender sends word up to the poor fellow with the tremens that he has a fine supply of the best whiskey that was ever in town, and that if he could just get down to his place of business he could fix him up all o. k. They don't seem to know that the poor fellow is already fixed up for a home in the pit.

As the poor fellow sobers up, his sins take another turn on him, and now they are like lead balls around his neck and are about to pull him into an awful hell. He sees no way out of his sins, and up comes the devil and says to him, "You are mine anyhow and if I were you I would just go in to have a good time while I did live; I have got you bound and you know it, and everybody else knows it. What is the use in ever trying to reform? You won't hold out a month. You know that you can't live a Christian if you were to try." And the poor fellow listens to the devil and says, "Well, that is so and I will never try again to do the right thing."

So he goes a little deeper into the life of sin, and now his sins are more like worlds than they are like mountains. He can't even see over the top of them. He can see over the top of a mountain, but here is a pile of sins that rises so high that no living man can see over the top of them. Now despair seizes him, and the next thing you hear of that man will be a funeral over in one end of the town. His sins were like a mountain, and at the last his sins were greater than all the others put together. He dies a murderer at his own hand, and goes out without one ray of hope.

A life of sin is like the awful storm cloud; it rises higher and higher and becomes blacker and blacker, and darker and darker, and at last it will burst through on the poor victim and sweep him off his feet, and sweep away every ray of hope and every vestige of manhood. Now love is gone, and honor is gone, and family is gone, and salvation is gone, and God is gone, and Christ is gone, and there is nothing in sight but the Judgment Day, and he is not ready for that. And the men who voted the license will give fifty cents each to bury him.

CHAPTER XX.

THE SIN THAT REJECTS GOD.

Dear reader, we have come to the place that it seems to us it would be the thing to take up the mountain-top sin in a broader sense, or get down to the root of the matter, and see just what the mountain-top sin is. And by the way, we feel led to say that in the dispensation of the Father the greatest crime that could be committed was to reject God the Father, and in the days of the Son of Man the greatest sin of that age was to reject the blessed Son of God, and under the dispensation of the Holy Ghost, it is to reject the Holy Ghost. So we find the three dispensations, that of the Father, and of the Son, and of the Holy Ghost. In order to get at the sin of all sins, we will have to take them up in their natural order, and if we do we shall see the mountain-top sin, and the sin that eclipses all other sins.

First, we will go back and look at the dispensation of the Father and see just what is the greatest sin in His age. Let the reader remember that Christ said all manner of sins should be forgiven unto man but the blasphemy against the Holy Ghost. Many people have wondered just what that sin was. Well, when I get up to it I think I can tell you just what it is, and I want to make it so plain that you will understand it all the rest of your life. Now we will go back and see what a fellow had to do under the dispensation of the Father to be a lost man. First, we will notice God's first warning to man. In Gen. 6:3, we read that "My Spirit shall not always strive with man." At a glance you can see that away back when this old world was young, that if a man acted in such a way that God's Spirit quit striving with him, that he was a lost man. Now let's look at a number of scriptures that show you that a man in that age could grieve God away until he was lost. In II Chron. 36:14-16: "Moreover all the chief of the priests and the people, transgressed very much after all the abominations of the heathen; and polluted the house of the Lord which he had hallowed in Jerusalem. And the Lord God of their fathers sent to them by his messengers, rising up betimes and sending; because he had compassion on his people, and on his dwelling place: but they mocked the messengers of God and despised his words, and misused his prophets,

The Sin that Rejects God. 135

until the wrath of the Lord arose against his people, till there was no remedy."

The reader will notice in the above text God did all that a gracious heavenly Father could do, but the people rejected Him and His prophets and rejected His messengers, and misused them until there was no remedy for them. Here was their trouble; they were under the dispensation of the Father, and their only hope of heaven was to go through the kindness bestowed on them by the Father. When they rejected Him and polluted His house, and turned their backs on Him, there was no remedy for them in the world.

It is like this: If I am in a deep pit and my only hope of ever getting out of there is in one man, and he comes to help me out and I deliberately reject him, you see at a glance that I am a doomed man, for there is no hope for me in the world. At a glance you can see the condition of these people. When they turned their back on God the Father until there was no remedy, what could they do but perish? The only way to heaven too was to go through the love and compassion of the Father, and they reject Him and turn away from Him, and as it were take the reins in their own hands and make shipwrecks out of themselves and their posterity. No more remedy for the crowd who rejected the Father while they were under His dispensation.

In connection with this lesson we will look at some more scriptures. We next notice Prov. 1:24-32: "Because I have called, and ye refused; I have stretched out my hand, and no man regarded; but ye have set at naught all my counsel and would none of my reproofs; I also will laugh at your calamity and mock when your fear cometh, when your fear cometh as desolation, and when distress and anguish cometh upon you. Then shall you call upon me, but I will not answer; they shall seek me early, but they shall not find me: for that they hated knowledge; and did not choose the fear of the Lord: they would none of my counsel, they despised all my reproof. Therefore shall they eat of the fruit of their own ways and be filled with their own devices. For the turning away of the simple shall slay them, and the prosperity of fools shall destroy them."

Now reader, it would take all of your time for the next ten days to try to go into details and explain this long quotation, but we can see at a glance that all of the above is a record of the people who rejected God the Father and were cut off from their hope of heaven. Under the dispensation of the Father, the only hope of heaven was to go through the Father,

The Sin that Rejects God. 137

And when a people rejected the Father, there was no hope for them, and they were cut off without a ray of hope to hang over their doomed souls, but darkness would settle down over them and they had no God. For when they rejected the Father there was no one else to take His place. They were hopelessly lost, for we hear the Father say, "Because I have called and ye refused, and I stretched out my hand and no man regarded, but ye have set at naught all my counsel and would none of my reproof, I also will laugh at your calamity and mock when your fear cometh."

This is one of the most fearful statements in the Old Testament. Of course I don't suppose that it literally means that the great God would really laugh at the damnation of a lost soul, but when the poor souls are passing out into outer darkness, and no hope in sight, and no God to call on and no one to lean on, and in the awful agony of the lost soul they call on God, but they have treated Him with such contempt that while they cry for mercy, God does not listen to their awful sad cry. They had their day, but said "No" to God the Father, and when they rejected God the Father the had no claim on the Son or the Holy Spirit. They were offered heaven by the love and

138 *The Sin that Rejects God.*

kindness of the Father, and they became God-rejecters.

In proof of the fact that they cut themselves off, we turn now and read in Jer. 7:13-15, "And now because ye have done all these works sayeth the Lord, and I spake unto you rising up early and speaking, but ye heard not, and I called you, but ye answered not; therefore will I do unto this house which is called by my name wherein ye trusted, and unto the place which I gave to you and to your fathers as I have done to Shiloh, and I will cast you out of my sight as I have cast out all your brethren, even the whole seed of Ephraim; therefore pray not thou for this people, neither lift up cry nor prayer for them, neither make intercession to me, for I will not hear thee." Now reader here is a class of people who grieved God and rejected God and acted in such a way that the Lord even asked the people to not pray for them, for He said, "I will not hear thee." Notice here just what He said about it: "Therefore, pray not thou for this people, neither lift up cry nor prayer for them, for I will not hear thee."

It would seem from reading the above text that a people can grieve the Lord until it is a real source of dissatisfaction to Him to even listen to anybody pray for them. The reader will remember that the Lord reproved Samuel,

The Sin that Rejects God. 139

the best man in Israel in his day, for mourning over King Saul after He had rejected him and removed him from the kingship of Israel. The Lord said to Samuel, "How long wilt thou mourn for Saul, seeing that I have rejected him from reigning over Israel." See 1 Sam. 16:1.

If the Lord can be so misused and mistreated and so rejected and so despised and set at naught and snubbed and laughed at and mocked that He will leave the man forever, and if it be distasteful to the Lord to even hear the man's name called, and all of the above scriptures say that it can, don't you see at a glance that the fellow is a doomed man? There is no hope in the universe for such a man. Just think of it, the Book says that a fellow can go so far that the Lord won't listen to his prayers and won't even listen to the man's friends as they pray for him. The Lord said don't even lift up cry or prayer for them or make intercessions for them, for I won't hear you. So you see the man has put himself out of God's reach, so far as love and mercy are concerned.

Now we are beginning to see what it means to sin against the Holy Ghost. A man can reject the Father until he is lost, and under the dispensation of the Father they did that very thing, and they were cut off in their sins without one ray of hope and without one glimmer of mercy left to them, and all you have to do to blaspheme the Holy Ghost is to treat Him in His dispensation as these people did the Father in His dispensation. No one act of sin is the sin against the Father, or no one act of sin is the sin against the Son, or no one act of sin is the sin against the Holy Ghost. But one continual, long drawn out stubborn rejection of the Father, settled it with them forever and ever; no hope in their skies.

Well now, we turn to the prophecy of Zech. 7:11-13, and read a few verses. "But they refused to hearken and pulled away the shoulder and stopped their ears that they should not hear; yea, they made their hearts as an adamant stone lest they should hear the law and the words which the Lord of hosts has sent in his spirit by the former prophets. Therefore came a great wrath from the Lord of hosts. Therefore it came to pass that as he cried they would not hear. So they cried, and I would not hear saith the Lord of hosts."

Now the reader will see a class of people here who the Lord said stopped their ears in order that they might not hear the law, and that they would not listen to the Spirit that was sent to them by the Lord through the former prophets, and he goes on to say that they made their hearts as an adamant stone. Now folks, don't you see that there is no hope for a man with his heart as hard as an adamant stone and his ears stopped? And at the same time He says of them that they turned away their shoulder; that is. they turned away with a kind of sneer and turned up the lip and turned up their nose and gave their head a toss and raised their shoulder as a sort of defiance to the God of Israel. And they refused to hearken, so the Lord says. We get a glance of them and we see at once that there is no hope, for they are in the dispensation of the Father, and the dispensation of the Son has not been inaugurated, and it is far off to the dispensation of the Holy Ghost, and the only one to deal with is the Father, and they have turned away from the Law and would not hearken to it; they have turned away from the prophets and will not hear them; and they have turned away from the Father, and will not hear Him, and have stopped up their ears and refused to hear, and have made their hearts as an adamant stone; so of course there is no hope.

Now what is to become of them?' Well, they are as much lost as if they were already in the pit. God is out of their thoughts, and of course if He is they are without hope. Don't you see that a man with a heart like an adamant stone can't think of feeling or loving or giving or shouting or praying? Don't you know that a rock can't do the service of the God of Israel? These men had become stones, and were rejected because they had rejected God.

CHAPTER XXI.

REJECTING GOD THE SON.

We have now come to the second stage of rejection. We are in search for the reason that men are lost. If God can't save a sinner (and we see that the sinner is not saved), there must be a reason for it, and the trouble must be with the man, and not with the Lord. In our last chapter we noticed that men rejected God the Father and were lost and now for awhile we want to see if we can find out why they were lost under the dispensation of the Son.

We all know that God loved sinners, and we all know that Christ died for sinners. Now if those are facts, and we all know they are, there must be a ground for God the Father and God the Son turning away from a lost man and turning him into an awful hell. But we read in John's Gospel 1:10, 11: "He was in the world, and the world was made by him, and the world knew him not. He came unto his own and his own received him not." Here is one key that will unlock the door and let you get a peep into the real condition of things.

Now reader, remember that the dispensation

of the Father is now past, and the dispensation of the Son is now inaugurated, and men now are to reach the Father through the Son. They can't go direct to the Father, for the Son is now the link between God and man. You come to Christ and ask Him how to get to the Father, and you hear Him say, "No man cometh to the Father, but by me; I am the door." That means if you get in by me you will have to come in by me and if you don't come in by me you don't get in at all. Then we have just read that He came to His own and His own received Him not; now reader, if He came to His own and His own received Him not, what is to become of them? The Holy Ghost has not yet been given, for the Son of Man has not yet been glorified, and the dispensation of the Father is now a thing of the past. The Father, so to speak, has had His day and age, and has passed off of the stage of action and has withdrawn Himself from the public and is now retired behind the curtains of time, and has put His well beloved Son on the stage of action. Now he waits to see whether or not we will receive Him, and with all the love of a great God and all the love of a tender Father, He watches to see just what we will do for we remember that when the Son was baptized at Jordan, the voice came from heaven, "This is my Son, hear him." And now it is hear Him or hear nobody, for the Father only works for us through the blessed Son.

Now if you will turn to the 4th Chapter of St. Luke's Gospel you will there have the record of the first sermon that the Son of God ever preached, and we will see just how they received it, and what effect it had on them, and see whether or not it was received or rejected. Please read the 28th and 29th verses. "And all they in the synagogue, when they heard these things, were filled with wrath, and rose up and thrust him out of the city, and led him unto the brow of the hill whereon their city was built, that they might cast him down headlong." If the only hope of heaven for these people is through the blessed Christ, and we know that it is, and here is the record of His first sermon, and they are filled with wrath and desire to drag Him from the synagogue to the top of the hill and cast him headlong, on what grounds do you think they will ever get to heaven?

It is to go to heaven through Christ or not go at all. What bright hope do you see in the future for that crowd? Their hope of heaven is in Christ, and now they have rejected Him, and not only that, but the desire of their hearts is to kill Him and get Him out of the way.

They watch Him and try every way in the world to get some clue at Him in order that they might put Him to death. No doubt but that they talked much of going to heaven; and what kind of a place would heaven be, if a set of murderers could get into it.

We read again in Matthew and Mark and Luke of the Master crossing the Sea of Galilee and coming to the country of the Gadarenes. There He found a man with a legion of devils in him, and we read that he was a terror to the whole country. He had broken jail and broken off chains and fetters and stayed out in the tombs, and cut himself with the stones, and he was so devil-possessed that no man could go where he was. The Master went over and saved the fellow, and when the people of the city came out the man was clothed in his right mind and was sitting at the Master's feet. It looks like the whole country would have gone forward for prayer. Well, let's see if they did. Read in Mark 5:17: "And they began to pray him to depart of out of their coast." Now the reader will see at a glance that there was no hope of that crowd on the face of the earth. They were lost. When the Son of God got into the boat there was a whole country of Christ rejecters as much lost as they can ever be.

Rejecting God the Son. 147

Again we read in the 12th Chapter of Matthew of a man whom the Lord God healed on the Sabbath Day, and now look at the 14th verse and you will see the results and the reward He got for His good deed. "Then the Pharisees went out and held a council against him how they might destroy him." Brother, or sister, you are a man or a woman of good judgment, and you know that these Pharisees were living at that time in the dispensation of the blessed Christ, and the only hope of heaven is in Christ, and now they have just gone out and held a council against Him that they might put Him to death. He has just said, "No man cometh to the Father but by me. I am the door," and what hope is there of those Pharisees? If they are not lost there is no such thing as a man ever being lost. So many people are concerned about the sin against the Holy Ghost. Well, it is enough to make a man tremble from the top of his head to the end of his toe. But while it is true, the man who sins against the Holy Ghost is a lost man, he isn't any worse lost than the man who sins against the Son of Man until the Christ has cut him off and appoint him his portion among the hypocrites and unbelievers. If a man cuts himself off from the Father or the Son or the Holy Ghost until he is lost, it don't change the thing a bit in the world which one he rejected. He is a lost man, and a lost man is a lost man, don't you see?

I could pile up Scripture here all day to show that the blessed Son of God was rejected, but you know it as well as I do. If you will turn and look at the betrayal of the Son of God by Judas and then look at His arrest and trial and conviction and see the mob on His trail as He was sent from the hall of Pilate to the hall of Herod, and see the awful mob and hear them shout "Let his blood be on us and our children. Give us Barabbas and let Christ be crucified." Get Him out of the way; we don't want to hear His preaching any longer. He says repent or perish, and we don't want to repent. He says, "Ye must be born again," but we don't want to be born again. He says, "Ye must be holy or ye can't see God," but we don't want to be holy, we want to be unholy, in fact, we are tired of Him; kill Him and get Him out of the way.

CHAPTER XXII.

REJECTING GOD THE HOLY GHOST.

We have now come to the scriptures that teach that a man may blaspheme the Holy Ghost and be forever lost. There is, and always has been and probably always will be, a great deal of talk about sin against the Holy Ghost, and thousands of people wonder by day and by night what the sin against the Holy Ghost is, and they seem to think it is some one act that they might commit and not know just what they had done and just when it was done, and finally be lost, but those are not the real facts in the case at all.

It is true that the Son of God says there is no forgiveness for the blasphemy against the Holy Ghost, but that don't teach that it is any worse to sin against the Holy Ghost than it is to sin against the Father. Here is the idea: There was a time when men dealt with the Father and were under His dispensation, and when they rejected Him they were lost, world wtihout end. Then the blessed Son of God came on the stage of action, and His dispensation began, and they rejected Him and were lost and went to hell in solid platoons. Then the Son passed from the stage of action and now the Father and Son in their council chambers of the skies arrange to give man one more chance, so they sent the blessed Holy Ghost into the world and He enters upon His dispensation.

Now think of it in this light: The Father has had His dispensation and has passed off the stage and sat down in His own council chamber, and the blessed Son came onto the stage of life and was rejected and put to death, and so He passed off of the stage of action, and now the Holy Ghost comes to the rescue of fallen man. Now, the only way to reach the Father or the Son either one, is by or through the blessed Holy Ghost. Don't you see at a glance if He is rejected and grieved and blasphemed that the man is left here in this world without one ray of hope? For the Father is gone, and the Son is gone, and now we have grieved away the Holy Ghost and He is gone, and the entire Godhead has been offended and rejected and there is no power in the universe of God to reach man's case. When we see the facts as they really are, we are not surprised to hear the blessed Son of God giving out these awful warnings to man not to sin against the Holy Ghost, for He knew that if they did that, they were lost forever.

Rejecting God the Holy Ghost. 151

We want to look at a few of the scriptures that give such awful warnings and see if we are right in our conclusions, and we think that we are. First, we look at Matt. 12:31. "Therefore, I say unto you, all manner of sin and blasphemy shall be forgiven unto men, but the blasphemy against the Holy Ghost shall not be forgiven unto men." Here is one scripture that shows if a man commits this crime or this sin he is a lost man, but don't you see that he is not any worse by sinning against the Holy Ghost than he was when he sinned against the Father until he was lost? Don't you remember that we have just showed you in one of the preceding chapters that the people sinned against the Father and rejected Him and mocked His prophets and shut their ears and made their hearts as an adamant stone? And the Book says that God's wrath was kindled against them until there was no remedy. Now in the above, we have the picture of a man sinning against the Holy Ghost until there is no remedy. Now reader, I ask you which one is the worst off if they are both rejected and both cut off from heaven and both are doomed to an eternity of night and despair? There is no difference in the two men in the world; both lost. One rejected the Father and blasphemed the Father until he was lost, and the other rejected the

Holy Ghost and blasphemed the Holy Ghost until he was lost.

But we turn and read some more scripture on this awful subject. We notice St. Mark's Gospel, 3rd Chapter and read the 28th, 29th and 30th verses. "Verily I say unto you all sins shall be forgiven unto the sons of men, and blasphemies wherewith soever they shall blaspheme, but he that shall blaspheme against the Holy Ghost hath never forgiveness, but is in danger of eternal damnation; because they said he hath an unclean spirit."

Now dear reader, because the blessed Son of God said in the above scripture that if a man blasphemed the Holy Ghost that he had never forgiveness, they seem to think that it was worse to sin against the Holy Ghost than it was to sin against the Father or the Son, and there are one or two passages of scripture that would seem to teach that doctrine, but if it was properly understood it don't teach it at all. But here is the idea: As we are in the last dispensation there is no hope of the man when he has separated himself from the Father and the Son, and now blasphemed the Holy Ghost. There is no way on the face of the earth for that man to ever get to God, for he has closed every avenue between himself and God, and is lost, because he has grieved away the Holy Ghost. Many good people seem to think that the blasphemy against the Holy Ghost is some one act that a man might accidentally commit and probably not know just what he had done, or just when he had the thing; but that is not the idea at all. Here is the real Bible meaning of the Scripture: The blessed Holy Ghost comes to the man and offers to take him to Christ, and lead him through the world, and lead him out of sin into eternal life, and the man deliberately rejects the blessed Holy Ghost and grieves Him away, and for the time being the Holy Ghost goes and leaves the man to himself. After a time He returns, and the man is convicted again, and this time the Holy Spirit struggles with Him, and the struggle is a desperate one, but finally the man is victorious and succeeds in driving the Holy Ghost away. Then he has hardened his heart much harder than it was before, and he begins to laugh at the idea of a preacher scaring him with the graveyard, or with his hell, as he calls it. Now he can sit up and tell you that no man can move him, and he seems to think that he is now much smarter than the average man, and is free from all these weaknesses that the average man is troubled with.

But the Holy Ghost hasn't given him up yet, and finally the blessed Holy Ghost comes to see him again, and the struggle is something awful. The man fights and the Holy Ghost struggles with him, and the man becomes so restless until he is afraid to go to sleep at night, and he wonders if he will have to yield. But the devil is there in all of his mighty power, and with all of his lies and deceitfulness he brings to bear on the mind of the man that it will ruin him for this world if he surrenders to Christ and there will be no more happiness for him in this world; that he will be all tied down with preachers, and that he can't go to the circus or the theatre or the race course any more if he gets religion. The devil is so shrewd that he makes that poor, deceived man believe that no worse calamity in the world could come on him than to become a Christian. The Holy Ghost struggles on and the man puts up the fight of his life, but finally the Holy Ghost says, "Well, I will let him alone. He is joined to his idols." That man comes out more than a conqueror and succeeds in driving the Holy Ghost away one time more.

Now just think of that man's condition. There is no way in the universe to make his case worse than it is. He can laugh now all he pleases at the weakness of his neighbors, but the man is doomed. He can walk about, but his face looks like a tombstone. Now he can tell you that he is beyond graveyard stories of the weak minded preachers, and as to their hell that they preach about, he takes no stock in any such stuff as hell and judgment days. The devil tells him that he has a long life before him and much happiness. He is not bothered with the preachers, has no trouble with the Spirit of God to dog his tracks, and he is a free man to do as he pleases. The poor man goes on as completely lost as if he were in the pit. The devil whispers to him that no preacher can scare him now, and the deluded soul chuckles in his sleeve that he has defied the God of heaven, and has rejected the Son of God, and the Holy Ghost don't bother him any more. Now he is delivered from all of this tomfoolery about getting religion, and he goes on to the Judgment Day a God-forgetter, and a Christ-despiser, and a Holy Ghost-rejecter.

Now brother, we have before us a man who has blasphemed the Holy Ghost and who is as much lost as if he were already damned. We have before us a man who is damned and is still above ground. There is no use in the world for you to tell the people that you don't know what the sin against the Holy Ghost is, for the rejecting of the Holy Ghost is without doubt the sin that we have heard so much talk about. Don't you see that the man is without one ray of hope, and don't you see that there is no power in the world now that can bring that man to God the Father, or to the blessed Son of God?' The Spirit is now grieved away and there is no power on the face of the earth that can reach that man's case.

Now we turn and read a lesson from St. Luke's Gospel, 12:10,, and you will see that it is the same as the rest. Notice how it reads: "And whosoever shall speak a word against the Son of Man it shall be forgiven him, but unto him that blasphemeth against the Holy Ghost, it shall not be forgiven." Here is the above idea: You may speak against the Son of God and find pardon, but when you have sinned against the Holy Ghost until He leaves you, there is no other court of appeal. You have cut the last shore line from the whole Trinity, and now you are drifting, and the longer you drift the further you go, and the harder you become, and the more you become like the devil in your heart and nature. Of course, when He said that if you speak against the Son of Man that it shall be forgiven, He did not mean to teach there that it was not a sin to do it, and a sin that will damn the soul if it is not repented of, for we read in the 9th Chapter of Luke and the 9th verse: "But he that denieth me before men shall be denied before the angels of God," so this verse shows us that we can't

Rejecting God the Holy Ghost. 157

sin against the Son of God and not pay the penalty, and shall suffer and forfeit our right to heaven. But the devil has been telling the folks for the last twenty-five years to my knowledge that the sin against the Holy Ghost was something altogether different from other sins, when right there in Luke's Gospel in the 10th verse He shows us that if we blaspheme the Holy Ghost that we are lost, and we think that is a great mystery, but right there in the same chapter and in the 9th verse He tells us that if we deny the Son of Man before men, that He will deny us before the angels of God. One is as fatal as the other. Here are the real facts in the case: Under the dispensation of the Father, if we rejected Him until He forsook us, we were lost. And a lost man is a lost man, it makes no difference if it was five thousand years ago or last year; the sin of rejection will have the same effect on the rejecter at any age of the world or in any dispensation.

We now turn to the First Epistle of John and read 5:16: "If any man see his brother sin a sin which is not unto death he shall ask and he shall give him life for them that sin not unto death. There is a sin unto death. I do not say that ye shall pray for it." Now reader, in the above scripture we have two classes of sin spoken of; one is the sin of wrong doing, which may be pardoned if confessed and forsaken, while the other is the sin against the Holy Ghost, which implies that the man has grieved away the Holy Spirit until He is gone. Of course if he is in such a condition as that, there is no use praying for him, for he has said "No" to the Spirit so often until the Spirit has left him and there is no hope for the fellow. John calls it the sin unto death, and of course we see at a glance that John is right.

When a man sinned against the Father until He left him, that man away back down the ages had done the same thing; he had sinned the sin unto death. But all sins are not of that character; a sin against the Lord may be forgiven, and a sin against the Holy Ghost may be forgiven, and a sin against your fellowman may be forgiven, but when any sin is persisted in until the Spirit leaves you, you are a lost man, it makes no difference as to what the sin is.

I believe a man can persist stealing cattle until God is so grieved that he is a lost man, or a man may persist in robbing trains and banks until that man is hopelessly lost, and I think that a man can persist in killing men until he is a lost man, and on the other hand I think a man might steal a cow and go to God and confess up to his crime, and pay the man for the cow, and go to heaven, the same as if he had committed any other crime. On the other hand a man might kill a man and go to God and find sweet peace and pardon and go to heaven shouting. But don't you see that is not the sin of persistent sin? Any of the above sins are sins of wrong doing and will damn as sure as the blasphemy against the Holy Ghost if persisted in and not forsaken, but they may be forsaken and confessed and repented of, and the man may find peace and pardon, and go to heaven a happy man. Any form of known sin is in violation of God's law and will damn the sinner if it is not repented of.

Now reader, we want to turn and look at a few scriptures in the Epistles of St. Paul and see just what he says about grieving the Holy Ghost. We turn first and read I Thes. 4:7, 8: For God has not called us unto uncleanness, but unto holiness. He therefore that rejects not man, but God who has also given unto us His Holy Spirit." In the King James version it reads that, "He that despises, despises not man but God," but in the Revised version it reads, "He that rejecteth, rejecteth not man, but God."

I quote the above to show you that a man may reject the Holy Ghost even after he is a converted man, and thousands of them have done it already. There is not a day but what some Christian repects the blessed Holy Ghost. Today if all the churches were to receive the Holy Ghost and let Him have His way with them, there would be nothing on the face of the earth that would be in our way, but we would sweep on and out beyond anywhere that we have ever been yet. Revivals would break out all over the land and the shouts of the saints would be something wonderful. The tidal waves of glory would roll all over this land of ours, and we would do more in the next few years than we have done since the day of Pentecost.

We turn and read another verse in this Epistle from the 5th chapter and 19th verse. It is not a long verse, but it tells as much as if it were ten feet long. Notice it: "Quench not the Spirit." Just four words, but it is a warning nevertheless, and sometimes the most awful and fearful warnings are not the longest. When the Lord says "Come," we had better come, and when He says "Go," we had better go, and when He says, "Whoa," we had better whoa. A warning is a warning, and as to the length of the warning, that has nothing to do with it at all. May you and I hear the voice of God, and when He says to us, "Quench not the Spirit," we had better not quench it for if we do we are as hopelessly lost as if we were already in

Rejecting God the Holy Ghost. 161

the tomb. There are plenty of men in this country whom the Lord can't do any more with than he can a dead man. A man in the tomb is no deader to the voice and will of God than plenty of living men, and yet they don't seem to be alarmed about their condition, and the people wonder and are amazed at it. Well, it is no mystery. A dead man never becomes alarmed; he is beyond the reach of the tender love of a loving heavenly Father. He is a dead man, and a bound man, and an entombed man, and a putrified man, and a man in that condition don't feel or desire to become acquainted with the great God who has done so much for him. It is all over with him now, for he has quenched the Holy Spirit until He has taken His everlasting flight.

We will turn to another scripture and see if we can get some more light on the subject. We now turn to Paul's letter to the Ephesians, 4:30: "And grieve not the Holy Spirit of God whereby ye are sealed unto the day of redemption." Here the Apostle tells us that we can grieve the Holy Spirit until we are sealed, and of course if that is true we see at a glance that a man can fix himself in such a condition that he is lost while he is still living. The Apostle gives a word of warning here to all men, both saint and sinner, and shows us in these few words that we, as sinners, may sin against the Holy Ghost until we are lost, and that the child of God may sin against the Holy Ghost until he is lost. The Holy Ghost has all to do with our salvation that is done here in this world. The office work of the Holy Ghost is to convict the sinner and lead him to the blessed Christ, and the work of the Holy Ghost is to lead the regenerated man to the Lord for the blessed experience of sanctification, and just as truly as the sinner can say "No" to the blessed Holy Ghost and pull back, the regenerated man can pull back and say "No" to the blessed Holy Ghost and keep that up until he *has* grieved Him forever away. Although he once was saved he is now lost and on his way to the pit of despair and the world of outer darkness.

But we will turn and see the reading of another scripture on this remarkable subject. We turn next to Acts 7:51: "Ye stiffnecked and uncircumcised in heart and ears, ye do always resist the Holy Ghost; as your fathers did so do ye." Here now, the martyr Stephen was talking to his murderers just before they had put him to death, and he charges them and their fathers of being guilty of the same crimes, that of resisting the Holy Ghost, and he called them the stiffnecked and uncircumcised in heart and ears, and said that "Ye do always resist the Holy

Rejecting God the Holy Ghost. 163

Ghost." He shows that they were a set of resisters, and a set of rejecters, and he said, ye always do this thing. Now that proves to us that they had other opportunities and that they had rejected them, and that they had kept it up until he called them a set of stiffnecked resisters. They had kept it up until they were case-hardened and sin-cursed and devil-ridden and hellbound. He said they were uncircumcised both in heart and in ears, and that they and their fathers had all been rejecters of God and Christ and the Holy Ghost. They are the same crowd that we read about in Hosea 5:6 and in II. Chron. 36:14-16, and Jer. 7:13-16, and Zech. 7:11-13, and Prov. 1:23-32, and many other scriptures that we could refer you to, but time and space will forbid it.

We can read the above scriptures and see what the Father had to contend with in His day, and then turn to the New Testament and see just what the Son of God had to contend with in His day, and now we have just read a number of scriptures to show that the Holy Ghost could be grieved, and that He could be resisted, and that He could be quenched, and that He could be blasphemed, and He could be sinned against.

Now I don't think I could make it any plainer than I have. Just keep in your mind that under the dispensation of the Father they could sin against Him until they were lost, and then keep in your mind that under the dispensation of the Son of God they could reject Him until they were lost, and now we are under the dispensation of the Holy Ghost and we can resist Him in the same way that they did the Father, and that He is very loving and tender, and easy to offend and to grieve, and that if we will obey Him and His blessed will that He will deal with us as tenderly as a mother will with her babe on her bosom. But if we turn Him down and grieve Him and resist Him and quench Him and drive Him from us we are the eternal losers and damned above ground. The Lord pity us. When the blessed Holy Ghost is forever gone, how sad the man and how horrible the condition. It would have been better for that man had he never been born. See what he has missed, and see what he has lost, and see where he is to stay all through a never ending eternity. Ho sinner! you may be drifting over the dead line tonight.

www.ingramcontent.com/pod-product-compliance
Lightning Source LLC
Chambersburg PA
CBHW031354040426
42444CB00005B/292